ANCHOR
BOOKS

A HARVEST OF MEMORIES

Edited by

Rachael Radford

First published in Great Britain in 2002 by
ANCHOR BOOKS
Remus House,
Coltsfoot Drive,
Peterborough, PE2 9JX
Telephone (01733) 898102

All Rights Reserved

Copyright Contributors 2002

HB ISBN 1 84418 016 6
SB ISBN 1 84418 017 4

FOREWORD

For many of us the medium of poetry offers us a voice - a voice to speak out and let others know what we feel, think and desire. It is the vital bridge of communication that lets us share our innermost thoughts and messages on life to people who may need that vital surge of poetic inspiration. It offers experience to those with none or little, spreads light to those in darkness and at the same time it encourages others that they are not alone.

A Harvest Of Memories is a unique collection of poetry written in a variety of styles with the theme of 'Down Memory Lane'. The poems are easy to relate to and encouraging to read, offering engaging entertainment to their reader.

This delightful collection is sure to win your heart, making it a companion for life and perhaps even earning that favourite little spot upon your bookshelf.

Rachael Radford
Editor

CONTENTS

Title	Author	Page
Solitary Imaginings And The Beech Tree	Jean Rosemary Regan	1
Memory Lane	K N Fordham	2
Dreams	Margaret Gurney	3
Bluebells	Linda Brown	4
Sunday School Treat	Sylvia Palmer	5
Bygone Days	David Walker	6
When I Was Young	Lesley J Marlor	7
My Memory Lane	Dorothy June White	8
Our Past Love	Irene Greenall	9
Pleasure In Old Age	Margaret Knox Stubbs	10
A Sound No Pilot Will Ever Forget	Louise King	11
Heptonstall	Wendy Kay Brandon	12
Melancholy Variations	Hugh Twose	13
Memories	Bernadette Mottram	14
Treasured Memories	Myra Bowen	15
High Rise Buildings	H Willmott	16
Friends Reunited	Mamorald	17
Fields Of May	Shirley Ann Kelleher	18
Young International	Edward Fursdon	19
Down Memory Lane	Vince Hughes	20
Remember	Rita Sackley	21
Remembering	Mair Wyn Cratchley	22
Last Visit	Sarah Smeaton	23
Knock Knock	Jean Streeton	24
An Infants Picture	Philip Beverley	25
When I Was Just A Lad	Jacqueline Bartlett	26
Sea Urchin!	Ann Odger	27
Loch Melfort!	Andrew A Duncan	28
Where Did I Go Wrong?	S Brown	29
A Scene From Childhood	Paul Wilkins	30
Pot Fair	G F Snook	31
A Memory	Mary Hughes	32
From Couple To Single	Carey Sellwood	33

Nostalgia - A Wartime Christmas	Pat Heppell	34
The Good Old Days	Pat Bradley	35
Smile A While	Lew Park	36
Our Wedding Day	Peter P Gear	37
Holiday!	Sue Umanski	38
Going Full Circle	A C Yap-Morris	39
Days Of Old	C Armstrong	40
Bluebells	Lesley Stockman	41
My Home Town	Sheila D Axton	42
At The Youth Club	Frank P Martin	43
Theresa - A Memory	Brian L Porter	44
Nostalgia	D Morgan	46
Childhood	Gary Redmond	47
Memories Of 1930's	M Macmillan	48
Memories Of Yesteryear	Alma Montgomery Frank	49
Down Memory Lane	Patricia Anne Turner	50
Down Memory Lane	Marie Barker	51
The Linchpin	Barbara Williams	52
Memories	D Sheasby	53
Street Football	M D Bedford	54
Down Memory Lane	Brian Akers	55
Sweetly Remembered	Betty M Irwin-Burton	56
A Winter Remembered	Margaret Hibbert	57
To A Queen Of Hearts	J Howling Smith	58
Once The Land Of Paradise	Fuchsia Coles	59
Santa's Getting Old	R J Ansell	60
Precious Things	Ellen Chaplin	61
Sunday School Outing	Joy Hall	62
When I Was Young	Harry Mason	64
Memorable Memories	Maureen Inglis-Taylor	65
Tabernacle Walk (The Early Years)	John Cook	66
I Wouldn't Change A Thing	L Smart	67
Seems Only Yesterday	John Wayre	68
A Balance Sheet Of Memories	Don Bishop	70
Grandma's	Parveen K Saini	71
Days Of Youth	Bessie Groves	72

The Eighties - A Decade Of Kaleidosocopic Memories	David Muncaster	73
A Village Summer	Mabel Barber	74
Yesterday	Katherine Parker	75
Down Memory Lane	John Townend	76
Thoughts From Memory Lane	Ivy Cawood	77
Whatever Happened To Vimto?	Adrianne Jones	78
Childhood Memories	Claudia Colella	79
Memories Are Made Of This	Joan Jeffries	80
Holidays With Grandma	V E Godfrey	81
The Field Day - 1937	Robert E Fraser	82
Dreams Don't Last Forever	Brandan G Ryan	83
Those Were The Days	Angela Pritchard	84
A Memory To Cherish	R E Weedall	85
Nostalgia	Jan Edmunds	86
Sundays	Joy Saunders	87
Blackberrying 1999	Joyce Preddle	88
Days Gone By	Joseph Broadley	89
Missing You	G Morrisey	90
The Little House	Eileen Phillis	91
A Thought Of You	P Evans	92
Whitsun Treat	Jean F Mackenzie	93
Christmas Past	S P Johnson	94
Memories Of Gran	Valerie McKinley	96
Step Back In Time	Pamela Eckhardt	97
Handstands	Linda Doel	98
Back To Then	Elizabeth Martin	99
Early Days At School	Kathleen McGowan	100
Once Upon A Time	William Hunt-Vincent	101
Early Days	Mike Fisher	102
Memories	D Adams	103
Life's Excursion	Marian Curtis-Jones	104
Down Memory Lane	John Paulley	105
Changing Years	Val Spall	106
Memory	Katy Sturman	107
Untitled	Roma Skrzypczak	108
Old Friends	Colin Boynton	109
Those Happy Days	Kate Strutt	110

A Sign Of The Times	Colin Spicer	111
From Time To Time	M U Stein	112
Looking Back	Charles Trail	113
Lost Years	S J Dodwell	114
Day Trips	Tom Usher	115
My Memories	I Foxcroft	116
First Meeting	Kenneth Copley	118
The Shambles	Bernice Sharpe	119
Reflections	Stephanie Henley	120
War Effort	Norman Bissett	121
Just Dreaming	S Kellett	122
My Childhood Days	Irene Morris	123
Childhood Memories	Margaret B Baguley	124
Now And Then	Maggy Copeland	125
Here's To The Next Time	D J Price	126
Childhood Memories	Vera Ewers	127
Radio Comedy From The Past	Dave Birkinshaw	128
Found	Elizabeth Taylor	129
Nan And Grandad's House	Joy Cooke	130
Memories Past	Margaret Hanning	131
Down The Ditches 1930s	Denis Pentlow	132
Ivy Cottage	Joan Chapman	134

SOLITARY IMAGININGS AND THE BEECH TREE

From vantage point of tall beech tree,
My world laid out for me to see.
Concealed among its branches high,
I viewed my kingdom, and by and by,
Childlike imaginings filled my view.
As ant-like neighbours, as if on cue,
Went about their daily tasks,
And filled my storyboard at last.
What adventures my imaginings wrought,
For unsuspecting neighbours, who sought,
Only to perform their daily tasks,
Unaware that in my mind at last
Their lives took on a heady glow.
What they would have thought, I'll never know;
But for me, from those dizzy heights,
Enclosed, and secret, out of sight.
Childlike and fond of those I saw,
Familiar, and maybe, most of all,
My world so safe and so well-known.
I could create scenarios for those at home.
All this was many years ago.
The beech still stands, I happen to know.
I wonder sometimes, if like me,
Another youngster climbed that tree,
Sat high upon that very branch,
And saw the sign I left at last.
'This tree is mine' I carved one day,
And hugged that tree, grew up; and went away.

Jean Rosemary Regan

MEMORY LANE

The meadow was a precious place,
A haven dressed in green,
The hours she had spent here,
Were the happiest she'd been.

The old oak tree was there still,
All gnarled and out of place,
'Just like me,' she thought,
And held a hand up to her face,

She did not see the new estate,
For her it was the same,
She only saw her one true love,
As they walked down Memory Lane.

K N Fordham

DREAMS

Happy memories are dreams that came true
With weddings, birthdays and reunions to name but a few
Happy memories linger to drive away the pain
Until we are united, together once again
The winter sun shines bravely to hide the dark cold days
Its warmth is all embracing if we stand within its rays
So keep a cheerful smile beaming on your face
And take the cold, cold world into your warm embrace
Dream of winter sunshine and of winter rain
Dream of autumn colours, forget sorrow and pain
Dream of sunny days, blue skies and sandy beach
And you will find your memories, all in easy reach.

Margaret Gurney

BLUEBELLS

A flower that I remember from my childhood
When I was taken in the magical bluebell wood
I still see the bells, in great abundance they grew
As I walked through the wondrous carpet of blue.

The bells hung and nodded in the gentle breeze
Whilst safely hidden in the shade of the trees
Their strong green scent filled the woodland air
That fragrance I still would love to share.

A sea of blue as far as the eye could see
Such a breathtaking sight especially for me
How I longed to pick them, but one mustn't dare
This heavenly beauty must always remain there.

Such an exquisite flower, this bell of blue
A shade of rich lavender, a kind of purplish hue
An upright stem surrounded by shiny leaves
Her meaning is constancy, this we can believe.

Long established in England, found in Elizabethan times
This lovely wild flower, a special favourite of mine
She will faithfully re-appear year after year
A flower so unique and loved most dear.

Many years since my childhood, the wood is no more
How I would love to visit just like before
But if I close my eyes, it's like a dream come true
Once again I am walking in the carpet of blue.

Linda Brown

SUNDAY SCHOOL TREAT

Every year we had a trip to the sea
The Sunday school outing to Burnham on Sea,
There was great excitement, as we piled on the old S + D
Dear Mum would be laden, with bulging straw bags
Brood of five, following behind, complete with name tags
We didn't have much, as kids we were poor,
So it was a touch of heaven, playing on the seashore
As the waves rolled in, we would splash in with a thud
And emerge a bit later all covered in mud.

How I loved the donkeys - especially Dolly,
Sister Bet, chose a mule, whose name was Polly
Why we thought it a treat, heaven knows
Bouncing up and down - sick and saddle sore.

Oh the love of the Punch and Judy show
Perched on the sand, right in the front row
Punch would give Jude, a hefty knock
Ding goes the cuckoo, in the clock.
Bang, wallop, Punch got his match - Jude lands him a clout
Us kids go bananas, we scream and we shout.
Four o'clock teas at Marchens - laid out in tea gardens
Trestle tables - and white paper clothes.
Hot sweet tea, under our noses would waft
Dundee cake - current bread, buttered buns
Looking back we sure had fun,
Grace before tea - I remember it well - all people who on earth do dwell
All agreed - what a wonderful day,
Except for poor old Mum, who had, had us up to here,
We would bawl our eyes out - as she chased us off the pier.
If I had a wish that wish would be
To go back to the 30's, and a day to Burnham on Sea.

Sylvia Palmer

BYGONE DAYS

If you saw me pass your cottage, and if you wondered why I smiled,
it was because of all the happy times I had there as a child.
My gran lived at Rosebud Cottage when I was just a lad,
and the holidays I had there were the best I've ever had.
In those days summers just seemed endless, I played the whole
                                                    day through,
but if it rained, and it sometimes did, Gran found me work to do.
I remember churning butter, baking scones, and shelling peas,
packing apples for the winter, and wrapping lumps of cheese.
I had a bedroom to myself, I was grown up now Gran said,
and she made a lovely patchwork quilt especially for my bed.
Every morning after breakfast we would go to feed the hens,
I would search around for eggs, while Gran cleaned out the pens.
Next, we would check the piglets, you should have heard them squeal
                                                    and grunt,
I had to feed one with a bottle, Granny said it was runt.
Alas, good times don't last forever, those halcyon days are gone,
but each time I pass your cottage, the memories linger on.

David Walker

WHEN I WAS YOUNG

Being the youngest child at home,
We didn't have a fridge, we didn't have a phone.
In the old house we had an outside loo!
Also we didn't have a bathroom too.
Remembering when we were children
We used to have fun,
Playing in the park on the swings and the slide,
Sitting on bread wrappers to make us glide!
Having a picnic with Mum,
Jam and sauce butties it was fun.
Searching in the brook for newts and frogs,
Running through the cornfield with Brandy my pet dog.
Making dens in the cornfield out of bales,
Telling the truth, never telling tales!
Playing with my dolls and my teddy bear,
Playing games like knock-a-door run, and do-a-dare.
Listening to music and buying 45s,
Having a crush on pop stars that came into our lives,
Day trips to Blackpool and Belle Vue Zoo,
Going to the Wimpy was the in thing to do.
Feather cuts and page boys was the hair style to be,
My hair was long and curly, hard to straighten you see.
I miss my turn-ups, smocks, tank-tops, and flares,
When I went to the youth club I used to get some stares!
Being with friends and family the good times we had,
Was it just a dream it makes me a little sad,
But one thing I have got is my teddy bear,
So I know it wasn't a dream,
But I wish I was still there!

Lesley J Marlor

MY MEMORY LANE

My memory lane is mine alone
Only I can go down
All on my own.
Only I find my way
Down this lonely track
For I alone know the long way back
Back to my childhood
Then on through years gone
Yes, they are behind me now
But I still need to hang on
For that was my lifetime
Be it sadness or tears
That was my lifetime
I have loved all the years.
There is still a way forward
We should all look to the front
But my own memory lane
Is something I'll always want.

Dorothy June White

OUR PAST LOVE

To me you are a Greek god, a warrior bold,
As the stories of our previous lives untold,
For when we recently met it seemed to me,
I would know you for all eternity.

Were you a soldier, emperor, lord, king or killer,
A philosopher, poets, noble man, blacksmith or miller,
Whatever you were many, many years ago,
I took your love, embraced it and never let it go.

It was taken from your hand, and I clasped it to my heart,
We loved and vowed we'd never be apart,
Since that solemn, heartfelt vow was taken,
I knew our love had previously lived and never been forsaken.

I met you and realised we'd been together long before
Your eyes full of love shook me to the core,
What was it about you that I recognised?
It seemed impossible our inmost thoughts could never be disguised.

From the past a beautiful haunting memory stirred,
Had my love upon you been conferred?
We met again and eyes betrayed the disbelief,
Our hears and souls entwined in ecstasy and relief.

We are destined to be together for always and forever,
The bonds of love are too strong to sever,
I know not what through the ages fate has decreed,
But this I know, from all bonds of separation we've been freed.

Irene Greenall

PLEASURE IN OLD AGE

From the activity of my mind
I find,
I may extract at will
My fill
Of magical memories made.

Now aged and reminiscing,
My wishful thinking
Brings alive
Friends and events to mind,
And find
Remembrance a timeless treasure.

Make memories while you may
For the day
Of lonely leisure,
Remember the old can survive,
Thrive and come alive,
Reliving life's precious pleasure.

Margaret Knox Stubbs

A SOUND NO PILOT WILL EVER FORGET

I walked across the Fenland fields
Wondering what a mid July day might yield.
The sweet smell of summer drifted away
As I rested in the hay.
Then out of the clouds came an amazing sight
Rumbling echoes of the Spitfire into flight.
Back at the controls was where I wanted to be
The heady smell of heather, euphoria rushed over me.
Dog fighting in the skies,
Memories of a day gone by,
Remembering friends and the ones which were lost,
Comradeship came at a very high cost,
She roared overhead with all her might
Then sadly faded out of sight.

Louise King

HEPTONSTALL

Sunday morning, a quiet hilltop village
Silent but for a few people
Wandering around
Among the gravestones
The home of my ancestors
I see my family name etched
On so many
Of those worn stones.
My mind drifts to distant days
I try to imagine their lives
In these ancient weaver's cottages,
It gives a warm feeling
To know that we are all linked together
In this chain of life.
I watch my little granddaughter Isabel
Dancing happily
Among the stones
'Grandma' she shouts
'Are those people all dead?'

Wendy Kay Brandon

Melancholy Variations

If I should live a hundred years before I lie
on Mother Earth in posture where I was to die
I think that I would keep awake
to see the melancholy morning break.
If yet another hundred years then I would try
upon the enigmatic morn to wake
to hear the curlew and the blackbirds cry.
Another hundred years amount to three
to delve upon the things there are to see
the all abounding transient beauty borne
upon the melancholy of the morn.

Hugh Twose

Memories

All the best memories
Are but a moment away
Brought to mind by something tiny
That illuminates our day

A smudge of paint on an old LP
A scratch in the groove of life
The record sticks at a certain place
And brings a flood of tears to mind

A certain smile, a special touch
Takes you back to another place
Reaching out through miles of time
To another someone, another face

A spoken word or a silly joke
Will stretch across the years
To bring back thoughts of yesterday
Like the purest of crystal, so clear

A tinkle of laughter heard from afar
Will make you smile unbidden
At the thought which pops into your head
A joyful memory not forbidden

All very the best memories
Are just a moment away
Brought to mind by something simple
That illuminates and brightens our day.

Bernadette Mottram

TREASURED MEMORIES

I remember Rhosneigr
The sandy-beached two-bay village
Where we took the children every year
To play in the dunes and build wondrous canals.

I remember the old lady who walked into the sea
Come hail, rain or shine because
Nothing would convince her that it did not
Do wonders for her rheumatism,
But I never knew her name or if it worked.

I remember the white-washed farmhouse
Where we always stayed and the weary trail
To the shore along the narrow dusty path
That skirted the willow-herbed and bull-rushed lake,
And the four rusty kissing gates over which
We had to lift our ancient pram.

We grumbled and grizzled, said never again,
But the sky was a perfect blue
And the sea as calm as a mill pond,
And there we joyfully returned
Year after year after year!

Myra Bowen

HIGH RISE BUILDINGS

There they stand these concrete pillars
Reaching for the sky
Ugly, soulless and depressing
Displeasing to the eye.

People live and people work
Inside their gloomy walls
Cut off from the outside world
As if they don't exist at all.

Where are the views that once we saw
Many years ago
Of church steeples and distant hills
And sunsets all aglow?

These monuments of man now block them out
And no longer do we see
Those distant views of yesteryear
Because of man's stupidity.

H Willmott

FRIENDS REUNITED

Friends reunited; what a blast!
Familiar names, from out of the past;
Where is she and where is he?
I wonder if they remember me!

The hardest part is the first approach -
The doubts and fears of stern reproach,
For losing contact, being out of touch,
'Did you think of us, very much?'

All in all, it's been worthwhile,
Though, between us, there's many a mile,
It's time to acquaint ourselves, anew,
With those whom, years ago, we knew.

Mamorald

FIELDS OF MAY

To capture the floating fragrance
from flowing fields of May,
dancing gleefully on the breeze,
softly lifting flowery fumed fay,
on warm lazy days.

I'm heartened by May's meadows
of fine, golden haze,
and her golden glow
fills my gaze,
with the first, flow
of springtime's graceful show.

Oh to walk amid your swaying
magical maze
with its earth steeped
in heaven's glaze,
among sun-scented meadows,
all so blissfully ablaze.

Then my mind's eye
would be blessed
as down Memory Lane
I'd be, in my field of dreams.
Among May's own mellow-yellow
good old days, captured on the breeze.

Shirley Ann Kelleher

YOUNG INTERNATIONAL

Once in my lifetime,
so I recall,
one couldn't keep moving around -
there were passports required,
visas to buy,
and frontiers dividing the ground.

Once in my lifetime,
so I recall,
children were seen and not heard -
with freedoms suppressed
and passions awry
of course revolution occurred.

Now in my lifetime,
I'm happy to tell
it's easy to travel afar -
just carrying a smile,
singing a song
and playing my passport guitar.

Edward Fursdon

DOWN MEMORY LANE

I remember the thrill of my very first kiss
With a head-turning, heart-stopping, nubile young Miss.
It came to me then as an almighty shocker,
That there's much more to life than a good game of soccer.

The school-leaving exams caused me much trepidation
So the news that I'd passed marked a milestone occasion.
It helped pave the way to another great day
When I found some employment and got my first pay.

In the Far East at eighteen, not a cause to rejoice,
Two years National Service, fit lads had no choice.
Many hardships, fine comrades, some memories quite sad
Of feeding poor children who had no mum or dad.

Another two years on and I had my first date
With the woman that I knew would end up as my mate.
A wonderful courtship then we walked up the aisle,
Over forty years later it still makes me smile.

I smile even more when I think of the joy
As I helped the young midwife deliver our first boy.
From then on having babies became quite a habit
As the fashion in those days was to breed like a rabbit.

Bringing up our four children was always a trial
But our happiness made it all feel so worthwhile.
With school plays and sports days and prize-givings too,
Many memorable holidays and trips to the zoo.

Along came family weddings with great jubilation
Soon surpassed by the birth of our new generation.
But what gives most pleasure, looking back on my life
Are the many tender moments that I shared with my wife.

Vince Hughes

REMEMBER

I don't remember like I did,
I hope you understand
My hair is not as curly as it was
In fact it's really got quite thin.

My figure is not as slim
Things don't fit as well
My shoes are flatter now
The colour of my clothes are not as bright.

But inside I remember everything
My hair is fair and thick
I still dance and sing
It's you, you see
Not me at all
That does not remember a thing.

Rita Sackley

REMEMBERING

The days of now that do unfold
I spend remembering those of old.
Of times just wandering in the sun
Of endless nights so full of fun.

Somehow the best of life is gone,
But once the world was mine when young.
I count such times and what I've done,
In thought I walk in misty sun.

The winter time seems darker now,
The wind is stronger, the trees they bow.
Long stay the nights, now it is late,
No one comes, yet here I wait.

Mair Wyn Cratchley

LAST VISIT

His eyes moved from the door I entered
To where I stood by his hospital bed
His feet hung out of the bed clothes
He pointed to them, I knew what this said
His socks were already on his feet
Anticipating the walk through the door
The pleasure of going home again
Illuminated his face as often before
Nothing could have convinced me to say
This time it will not be so
I then resolved to stay beside him
Let him be the first one to go
That day he went home to the Lord
From pain and suffering set free
I returned home a widow
But the Lord came also with me.

Sarah Smeaton

KNOCK KNOCK

Every day it was the same,
Early morn the milkman came,
Baker then brought bread for toast,
At mid-morning, came the post,
Once a week, a lorry called
So our coal could be installed,
Our insurance man would knock
Once a month, at six o'clock,
In between, we had lots more
Salesman standing at our door,
In their cases, plastic mops,
Cheaper than those in the shops,
Dusters, brushes, polish too,
All displayed for Mum to view,
Weekly visits from the 'pools' -
'Pay your money, read the rules.'
Every year it was the same,
But my daddy never came.

Jean Streeton

AN INFANT'S PICTURE

Miss Lees, Miss Lees, oh sweet Miss Lees
Who took us on nature rambles
Looking at butterflies, harebells, huge oak trees.
There never were any preambles.

Sweet, dark-haired Miss Lees who'd been
All the way to Africa;
Who showed us the slides of things she'd seen
And the souvenirs she'd brought back with her.

She had me hold up my pictures before the class
And lavished them with so much praise,
I took oh so for granted all the exams I'd pass.
(Too bad fate led me along other ways).

And when we played 'Mousy Mousy, can we
Come into your little wee housy?'
I would be the one as snug as can be
Under Miss's desk playing 'Mousy'.

So whatever became of dear sweet Miss Lees
Whose nature was harebells and sweet vernal grass?
She, without setting essays, showed us landscapes and trees.
I'd love to say 'thank you' but fear I'm too late, alas!

Philip Beverley

WHEN I WAS JUST A LAD

Over the hill and far away
I went wandering one fine day
I went with hat on the back of my head
And a blanket rolled up to make my bed.

I really meant to camp outside
To enjoy myself and take a ride
And
Far, far away
I went that day.

The sun was high in a sky so blue
Not a cloud in sight - but alas who
Did I see at the top of the hill
But my aunt Alice and a man called Will.

She did not seem pleased to see me at all
And in watching her - I hit a wall
I lost my hat and it went quite flat
I lost my lunch and that was that!

My blanket fell with a horrible thud
Into a place with the thickest of mud
Aunt Alice and this man called Will
Were no longer on the hill,
I looked around
Until I found
Them cuddled upon the ground.

When the sun went in and down came the rain
I thought I'd return to my home again,
But I never saw my aunt again,
They told me she'd got fat and had a pain
I thought perhaps could it have been the rain?

Jacqueline Bartlett

SEA URCHIN!

When I was young, I can recall
jumping the gap in harbour wall,
reaching as far as I could go,
looking down at the tidal flow.

Feeling the spray upon my face
from waves hitting the concrete base.
Knowing the danger standing there,
easy to slip, so must take care.

The sense of power of the sea,
filling my soul, a part of me,
the rising tide soaking my feet,
weather changing to rain and sleet.

Time to return with heavy sigh,
watching each step, the tide so high,
re-crossed the gap, then looked below,
watched the waves pounding to and fro.

Safe on the beach, but cold and wet,
exciting day I won't forget.
It's good to think of times now past,
fond memories are made to last.

Ann Odger

LOCH MELFORT!

Tis good fortune to be born alive
in springtime of the year
when everything that nature knows
gives welcome to you here.
The air is cool, but nicely so
in Melfort's favoured spot
while sun and warmth
can equally give
a welcome - very hot.
So lucky have we been to date,
twice favoured in our lot
to spend a time in leisured ease
in Melfort's golden plot.
On looking back o'er many years
of pleasure, sadness too
we thank our God for favouring us
with nature's radiant mood.
Tis good as well, to know the place
transcending worldly cares
while one is left with memories fond -
the answer to one's prayers!

Andrew A Duncan

WHERE DID I GO WRONG?

Why are my days so empty, why are my nights so long?
What happens now I wonder, where did I go wrong?
What happened to the good times, the joy and all the laughter?
What happened to the story and the happy ever after?
What happened to the sunshine, the music and the lights?
What happened to the crazy days and warm romantic nights?
What happened to the dancing, the singing and the charm?
What happened to the energy, why did it turn so calm?
What happened to the parties, the picnics and the beach?
What happened to the life I know, why am I out of reach?
What happened to the caring, the warm and loving touch?
What happened to life's meaning, why did I lose so much?

S Brown

A SCENE FROM CHILDHOOD

The tree trunk in our wartime imagination
Is a bomber
And we are the crew
Branches are machine guns
Which we fire at
Imaginary
Messerschmitts
Focke Wulfs
Or Japanese Zeros
As we watch our model aeroplanes
Streak into winter air
On broad balsa wings
Or hedgehop daisy hillocks
Spitting and trailing white model jet engine smoke.

Paul Wilkins

POT FAIR

Each summer potters and auctioneers would come to town,
with every type of pot you could ever need.
Baskets of pots with many colours,
Auctioneers throwing pots from hand to arms,
juggling them about,
to attract a crowed.
A loud voice would say 'Who will give me a fiver for the lot?'
Half a dozen hands would shoot up in the air,
all trying to get their bargain while they can,
What an attraction for a young child.

G F Snook

A MEMORY

I remember when I loved you,
It was so long ago,
For now there is only silence,
That follows where I go.

It was just imagination then,
Well meaning friends all say,
But I remember otherwise,
Yet let them have their say.

The echo of your voice remains,
With joy I hear it yet,
The words are all so very clear,
I never shall forget.

Mary Hughes

From Couple To Single

Good friends they're all I need
I tell myself to succeed
The evening goes
The drink flows
And the laughter shows.

My thoughts drift to you
I drag them back
I am alright
I have to fight
I can get through the night.

You're just another person
The same as all these here
Fix my mind
On their kind
I'm leaving you behind.

Music's playing and
I find myself trying
To believe it's true
With someone new
I'm surviving without you.

Carey Sellwood

NOSTALGIA - A WARTIME CHRISTMAS

In the chill darkness, I finger the telltale bumps,
An orange, some crinkly walnuts make the lumps
In a worn, woolly sock ribboned in red,
Tied to the brass knob at the end of my bed.
Much too early to light my stub of candle,
Gingerly, I creep to the door, turn the handle.
A gnawing cold fills the stone-floored house,
I shiver and scurry like a mouse,
Back to the snugness of my mattress of feathers,
A welcome cocoon in the wintry weather.
For days the postman has trudged through the snow
Bringing cards and letters from friends we know
Back in the city, where bombs forced us to flee,
My mother, brother and I, now evacuees
With an elderly aunt in her cottage of thatch.
Now, a stirring, steps on the stairs, a lifted latch.
At last Christmas day has begun!
Now for some breakfast, a few presents, some fun.
At the wooden table, cups set out for hot tea,
Small piles of presents for my brother and me.
A Girls' Crystal book, a diary, a fountain pen.
My brother has a Rupert annual, a fire engine with men.
Iron pots on the black-lead stove begin to spit,
One holds the Christmas pudding with threepenny bits!
There's a plump farm chicken with sage and onion stuffing,
Everything on ration, yet we lack nothing,
Fresh grown vegetables, a boiled carrot cake,
Paper chain decorations, Mother helped us make.
After tea, carols on the wireless, Christmas day's been fine,
A game of cards, then cocoa, into bed by nine.

Pat Heppell

THE GOOD OLD DAYS

Cobbled streets and paraffin lamps
Penny loaves as well
Rag and bone man on his cart
With donkey stones to sell
We washed our clothes in dolly tubs
And used the posser too
Then squeezed them through a mangle
And rinsed in dolly blue
Ladies wore black stockings
Whilst working at the mill
Paraffin lamps were used indoors
To take away the chill
Tin baths were used for bathing
The outside loo was cold
There was no central heating
In the days of old
There was no television
Sometimes it was quite bleak
So we played hop-scotch, top and whip
Skipping, hide and seek
The old days didn't seem so bad
Compared with things today
No muggings, killings, terrorists,
Just children safe at play.

Pat Bradley

SMILE A WHILE

Why don't you smile anymore?
What is the reason for this?
Are you resting on some distant shore . . . or . . .
Is it the soft touch of a kiss?
Can you remember holding hands . . .
Strolling so aimlessly on rippled sands?
Does your soul reach out for the days, long gone?
Do you hear the faint echo of 'Love's Old Sweet Song?'

You see, dear one, I have memories too,
And . . . I confess, they all centre on you but
The past is past, and so long ago,
And the memories we have, are all there is to show,
So back to the now
The present is here
The future tomorrow
Go forward, my dear . . .

Lew Park

OUR WEDDING DAY

The register was signed
Side by side we vowed ne'er to part
And sung the hymn
'Oh Lord, how great thou art.'

We have grown to love each other more
With every passing day
Our love it goes from strength to strength
As we travel life's highway.

We give and share this love we have
That draws us so close together
And we know no storm will ever drive us apart
No matter what the weather.

Our life, our love, cannot be bought
Nor can it be sold
Our promise at the alter it is so safe
And never will unfold.

Our families and closest friends
Where there that lovely day
To witness our wedding
On the fifth of February.

Peter P Gear

HOLIDAY!

Sun shining
Warm on my face
Beach reminder
A fantastic place.
Sandy ice cream
Paddling feet
Burying Dad
Sandwiches to eat.
Gritty toes
Shovelling spades
Riding donkeys
Those were the days.

Sue Umanski

GOING FULL CIRCLE

Memories return to haunt me, enchant me.
Life has its magic moments, bitter ones too
Retracing steps along life's highway
Which are the memories you would cling to, which erase?
Ecstatic, passionate moments with bitterest taste?

Fun times, mad times, with agony, with pain.
Laughter on cloudy days when you learned to put things right again.
Differences are patched up by close of night
No matter how we argued you'd put things right.

Would you banish the frivolous things you thought you'd never do?
The world had an open gate that welcomed you
You savoured temptation, made mistakes
I'd forgive you, make excuses, cover up for both our sakes.
No love was lost between us, life's an eternity with you.

A C Yap-Morris

Days Of Old

In days of old when I was bold
I played a knight in shining armour
I made my brother stand his ground
As I charged at him. What drama!

I draped a sheet around my horse
And a hood to cover his head
I galloped up with spear in hand
To kill my brother dead.

I couldn't understand. He moved
When ready for the kill
I saw him running for all his worth
To the gate on top of the hill.

C Armstrong

BLUEBELLS

Through the woods I used to go,
Along the winding narrow path,
Where the bluebells used to grow
I'd sing and dance and sometimes laugh.

Then along the track I knew,
The JCB came digging deep,
Where the scented bluebells grew,
Buried bulbs in endless sleep.

Now motorways roar in full flow,
The tarmac ribbon unwinds ahead,
Where the bluebells used to grow;
Where I can no longer tread.

Not this paved road but carpets blue,
No grinding lorry, hurtling car
Where the woods of bluebells grew;
Not just a memory from afar.

Oh, how I wish for time to slow
And backwards run until it cease
When the bluebells used to grow,
When I can rest at last in peace.

Lesley Stockman

MY HOME TOWN

I was born in Battersea
In dear old London town,
The house I used to live in
Has long since been pulled down,
The sweet shop on the corner
Has gone with all the rest,
And when I look at all the flats
I'm really not impressed.

The factory that I worked in
Was just across the way,
We'd listen in to 'Housewives' Choice'
As we packed sweets all day,
And at the Totters Barrows
On Saturdays we'd stop,
Or go and look for bargains
At Curly's second-hand shop.

The cafe that we went in
Was down the Falcon Road,
We used to go in for our tea
And maybe sausage toad,
The folks who used to own it
Their names were Bill and May,
The cafe's now a block of flats
And they have moved away.

I'll not forget old Battersea
The station and the trains,
Prices candle factory
The smell of rotten drains,
The factory that we worked in
Like the houses now is gone,
But the memory of those happy years
Will always linger on.

Sheila D Axton

AT THE YOUTH CLUB

Back years ago at the Bar Two Thousand,
People came from all around.
Disco sound and rock and roll,
Funny dancing and the stroll.

Greasy Frank playing disco sound,
People rocking all around.
Steppen Wolf and Born to be Wild,
'Status Quo play the B side'.

With mini skirts and leather jeans,
Dig it out at the local scene.
Summer days and balmy nights,
'Let's go rocking turn out the lights.'

Liquid wheels shone around,
To add effect to the disco sound.
Back when the sun did shine,
Lots of fun a super time.

Bikers with their leather wear,
Flower power in the air,
Hippies in their caftans,
When tie-dye was in fashion.

Frank P Martin

THERESA - A MEMORY
(Thornwick Bay, Flamborough, 1967)

We met beneath a holiday moon, arranged to meet next day at noon.
We walked and talked, we combed the beach, skipped breaking waves,
keeping just out of reach.
We watched the seabirds overhead, I remember,
your skirt was fiery red.
And all the world was just a game, and each of us knew,
we felt the same.

Time stood still, at least, we thought, the ways of love,
each other we taught.
The fleetest touch, a featherlight kiss, holding hands in youthful bliss.
Walking together, the world shut outside,
for what we felt was deep inside.
I was fourteen, so were you, the sun shone bright, the sky was blue.

And as evening stretched into the night so the moon cast its glow
on our teenage delight.
But with the coming of each new day, so grew shorter our holiday stay.
Until the time came, when we had to part, and we both felt
a deep wrenching, a pull in the heart.
We said a tearful last goodbye, I tenderly kissed each red rimmed eye.

Would we ever meet again? We thought we would, but that was then.
I said goodbye, waved as you left, and my youthful heart was
broken, bereft.
And now the holiday was done, no more evenings with you,
no more walks in the sun.
Home once more, back to daily existence, yet your memory remained
with dogged persistence.

Time marches on, time we must live, we love and we suffer,
we take and we give,
Yet, somewhere inside, there's a part of my heart, that seems
to remember when it all seemed to start.
So many years have passed and yet, I remember you still,
and the day we first met.
Theresa, Theresa, I still remember your name, do you remember
me too, my heart's first true flame?

Brian L Porter

NOSTALGIA

Memories of childhood
In East End's Bethnal Green.
Rows of little houses
No longer to be seen.
A three roomed terraced our abode
Which eight of us did share
The concrete backyard where we played
Was just a few feet square.
Mother took in washing
To help to make ends meet
She stood for hours and hours
On her poor old swollen feet.
With sunlight soap and rubbing board
She battled with the loads,
The mangle was a godsend
For wringing out the clothes.

The iron pot upon the hob
The kettle black with soot,
The iron fender on the hearth
Where boots and shoes were put.
The copper in the corner
With a fire down below
That heated water for our needs
Laboriously slow!
Chestnuts roasting, bloaters sizzling,
On a grid iron o'er the fire,
Nostalgic thoughts of childhood
Help lift my spirits higher!

D Morgan

CHILDHOOD

Do you remember day after day
Spying on birds' nests and romping in hay
Fishing for rud along Merricks' lake
Scrumping the apples, posh village fêtes?

And what about milk with the solid gold crown
Trees in the school yard, we'd climb up and down
Beach trips and parties, choral events
Anatomy lessons for twenty new pence?

From town centre discos we'd bop round and dance
To first tell tale signs of a whirlwind romance
With the last of the corner shops, wafer ice creams
Said farewell to our childhood of effortless dreams.

Gary Redmond

MEMORIES OF 1930S

Board the steamer at bridge wharf,
 Sails down the river, Govan first stop,
'Twas most exciting, fore and aft,
 Watching shipyards passing, all agog.

On the steamer we had such fun
 Running around, one deck to another,
Looking in amazement the big engine turn
 Brass bright clean a'shining, oh mother.

Those memories stay in my mind
 Of the great big engine, acting as one,
Up over round and down, not a grind,
 Then kept doing the same, all over again.

This is what made the big paddle turn
 Making the steamer, glide right on,
With a great whoosh of water, and glinting sun,
 Right down the Clyde, by Dumbarton.

Stopping at Greenock and Weymms Bay,
 Sail over the mouth of the estuary,
Into Kirn and on to Dunoon
For our summer holidays, which end *too* soon.

M Macmillan

MEMORIES OF YESTERYEAR

How great were yesteryears
No hurry, time to think
Days of happiness with one's brothers and sisters
A laugh a minute and a time to drink

Spring would come in with her multicolour coat
Bluebells glittering around the old apple tree
Daisies shooting up around the family goat
One at all times felt extremely free

Summer was a happy leisurely, noble time
When all creation laughed and sang all day
Work was done at a slower mime
And one loved each day in a divine way

Autumn slowly appeared from nowhere
The colours of the flowers and leaves looked divine
Even humans took their time to prepare for the
Fine end of the autumn fair

Icy cold days were always there
Snow galore prepared the soil for wonderful crops
Sledging, sliding and spading to make Father Christmas
Whoever made him, he always looked his best with his
    coal eyes, nose and mouth as his props.

Memories will never fade
Each new year they spring to light
And raid one's lives in their greeny jade
We love to remember with all our might

Alma Montgomery Frank

DOWN MEMORY LANE

Remember the days you could run to the shops
Without the need to take Ma or Pops
The streets were as safe as houses.
The fashions were strange
Oh my! How they've changed
Since the days of the bell-bottomed trousers.

The number of sweets you could buy for a shilling
Fruit salads and black Jacks that pulled out your fillings
D'you remember Bazooka Joes?
With the pictures inside
You could send for a prize
Ah! Where did those years go?

The hours were spent playing hopscotch, or balls
In the courtyard outside, or up on the walls
Or we'd knock up the neighbours and run
Oh! Those were the days
When kids knew how to 'play'
And we sure knew how to have fun.

The TV was crammed with robbers and cops
And we also enjoyed 'Top of the Pops'
We'd scream when the Osmonds came on
The soaps were so neat
Like 'Coronation Street'
And that one is *still* going strong!

Now, times have changed. The years have been many
And the coin in my pocket's a pound, not a penny
But I feel it all went so fast!
So I often recall
The times I was small
Because memories are meant to last

Patricia Anne Turner

DOWN MEMORY LANE

I remember the Sunday mornings at Sunday school
Where we sat round a tallish fire
Whose chimney went through the roof!

It kept us warm
Mr Edwards used to open the lid
And poke the fire to life
Then there was a glow of warmth
All round the circle!

We heard and listened to the Bible!
All six of us in our best clothes.

Marie Barker

THE LINCHPIN

The Queen Mother was the linchpin
Of our Royal Family
Firm but gentle attitude
Gave much needed stability
Whilst common-sense and fairness
With love and caring grew
To world-wide appreciation
Of the gracious one we knew
Perhaps her greatest asset
Was enthusiasm for life
Which joined service for her country
To mother and loving wife
Women in our present times
Might care to ponder this
Her quiet gentle ways
Did more to promote the rights
Of women in our nation
Than all the militant efforts
Of the fighters for liberation
Her legacy of service
To the monarchy and us
Always a shining beacon
Royalty without fuss

Barbara Williams

MEMORIES

I sit alone and wonder
Why it should be so
That I hear so clearly voices
From pasts so long ago.

Little laddies a-shouting
Who must be retiring men
Little lassies laughing
Who will never see sixty-one again.

I hear the songs of fishermen
Sailing out to sea
Melodies that dance bands play
When I was twenty-three.

Hymns the choir practised
In the centre village hall
Songs we sang when playing ball
Against the schoolhouse wall.

I hear the village old folk
Long sleeping in the grave
Talking of the good old days
Recall the good advice they gave.

Maybe it's my mind that's gone
Now I'm ninety-three
I'd better rise up and stir myself
And make a lovely cup of tea.

D Sheasby

STREET FOOTBALL

Down inside our road
Between kerb and lamppost
There I say we had
Three yes football pitches
Boy was I the lucky one
For mine was in the middle
The other two for friends
Mine was near my home
But if I played away
Home in time for tea *still*
I'd even run in quick
Yes if it started raining

M D Bedford

DOWN MEMORY LANE

Idyllic days by the river bank,
Stick and string and bent pin, into the river sank,
Outstretched arms when I came home,
Never left on the street to roam,
Memories of Mr Porter with his horse and cart,
Fruit and veg gave us a good start,
Brass scales with small shiny weights,
People waiting for Mr Porter at their front gates
Dad with coal dust face coming!
Mum saying, 'Don't touch the tablecloth,
It's not becoming.'
On the woodland with friends and dog!
Lazy days on woodland logs,
Memories of aircraft bombing,
Down the air raid shelter,
Quick they're coming!
Memories of my infant school,
Prefab buildings with cast iron fires,
If we were cool!
Four sisters and a lovely brother,
Graced with Father! And a wonderful mother.

Brian Akers

SWEETLY REMEMBERED

It was another world away
The war was yet to come
There were unsullied skies of blue
Warmed by an English sun.
The fields were full of buttercups,
Wild rabbits played quite near.
As a child I wandered down the lane
With nothing there to fear.
Hedges filled with May blossom
Brought sweetness to the air,
The milkman's horse enjoyed its taste
As it stood and waited there.
A gill of cream, a pint of milk
All came from cans and cart
And tasted fresh as nectar
As it gave the day a start.
The skylark sang all day above
The fields beyond the stile,
And a herd of cows stood watching as one ran
From school the homeward mile.
The changing seasons - all were seen
And delighted every eye,
But all is brick and concrete now.
No lark sings in the sky.

Betty M Irwin-Burton

A Winter Remembered

It froze hard that year, frost was everywhere,
On the gardens, the rooftops, in the trees
And even in those dark sheltered places where
Nothing grew. And so still, so still, no breeze.

It froze hard that year, I remember rose-tinted skies
And fields made bright by the white
Of the frost and the pond turned to ice where
We came sliding and playing in the light -

Of those short rosy winter afternoons,
Our laughter ringing through the frosty air
As we slid and chased across that icy floor
With warm flushed faces forgetting that soon

The fading winter light would send us home.
I remember still; it froze hard that year.

Margaret Hibbert

TO A QUEEN OF HEARTS

From dust we come
Like blades of grass
We shoot and bloom
Then fade.

A hundred and one years
Have disappeared
As fleeting moments
Now death has reared.

So many sweet memories
Left hither and away
Many reside around
The 'Castle of Mey'.

Your love for a child
Gentle and kind
Showed compassion to him
With that void in his life.

Your love for your king
So constant and true
To lose him so early
A cruel blow for you.

But - you carried on
Gave your realm your devotion
The thought to give in
Was never a notion.

Dearest Queen Mum Elizabeth
Now at rest from all trials
We will never forget
Your face and your smiles.

J Howling Smith

ONCE THE LAND OF PARADISE

I was walking in China Town in Piccadilly.
Perfume wafted to me on the breeze. Was it a lily?
Then it dawned upon me - Burma's 'Venison Bud'!
Memories came back to me in a flood!
Exotic frangipani, fragrant flower with heart of gold;
creamy petals tipped with pink.
Into its heart my nose I'd sink.
Mangoes dangling from the trees.
Temple bells tinkling in a vagrant breeze.
Sail boats passing down the Irrawaddy river.
Midday sun makes the molten water quiver.
Gul mohur on the tree tops flame,
living up to its English name -
'Flame of the Forest'. Gold of *Padauk*
decorate the roads during the Water Festival.
Demure maidens looking for their 'Percival'.
Saffron-robed monks with ebony bowl,
for a handful of rice will pray for your soul.
Once it was the 'Land of Paradise',
now I remember her with tears in my eyes.

Fuchsia Coles

SANTA'S GETTING OLD

When I was a child from five to fifteen
I lived in a London which wasn't too clean.
The smog from the coal fires, thick, green and grey
And the crunch of the snow came before Santa's sleigh.

The warm syrup sun dried the tall common grass
As my lead soldier army held the back garden pass.
We played in the churchyard with a goal drawn in chalk
For those few golden years I could make the ball talk.

My pleasures were many my problems were few.
I remember no rain only skies that were blue.
Like old photographs the memory's edge haze
But I know in my heart that they were better days.

Now at fifty or more I live somewhere not home.
Not bad but not magic I've learned how to roam.
The mist is just wispy the snow is just cold
And Santa like me is just grey, fat and old.

My head's full of facts my heart's broken but wise
And my soul seeks a way out from behind my tired eyes.
The body sits broken like the lead soldier's frame,
The ball control's gone I just talk a good game.

These days the blue skies are watery thin.
That young boy has aged now but still lives within.
At the end my last memory gentle and sweet,
A small child at play on a warm London street.

R J Ansell

PRECIOUS THINGS

Precious things, precious things,
The moments of magic with gossamer wings,
They stay not long but take their flight,
Out of sight, out of sight.

Out of sight, but fresh in mind,
Are the memories they leave behind.
Memories that give us pleasure,
The precious things we'll always treasure.

Ellen Chaplin

SUNDAY SCHOOL OUTING

For our Sunday school treat, we've waited a year
We have saved all our pennies and now it is here,
My three friends and our kids
On the train to Hunstanton which we did.

Sandwiches, bathing costumes and towels we took
It was a thrill to be on the train and look,
To see the fields roll by and then we
At last, hooray! We can see the sea.

Off the train we all did trot
Just hope we hadn't forgot,
To leave anything on the train
Macs and umbrellas in case it does rain.

Down to the sea did the children run
Spades and buckets to dig in the sand,
Come on you lot!
Sandwiches and pop is what we've got.

After, we went and paddled and had fun
Some sat quietly in the sun,
We then got dressed and dried there
And packed our bags and went to the fair.

Sixpence for rock, threepence a ride
And the ghost train we went inside,
Then all the children we had to find
To catch the train and not leave behind.

We had to stand in the corridor
Some of the children had to sit on the floor,
We are all so tired and thankful to be here
And save up for our Sunday school outing next year.

I remember this Sunday school outing with my friends
and the children, we looked forward to going every year
It was great fun and a laugh.

Joy Hall

WHEN I WAS YOUNG

When I was young, I used to knit,
And knit, and knit and knit, and knit,
But nowadays, I must admit,
I know I'll never finish it.

When I was young, I used to read,
And read, and read, and read, and read,
Its contents I still read with rapture,
And soon - I'll be finishing, the first chapter!

When I was young, I used to walk,
And walk, and walk, and walk, and walk,
But now I am old, it's plain to me,
I can no longer walk from A to B.

Harry Mason

MEMORABLE MEMORIES

A glowing, shining day of spring,
This special day mixed thoughts will bring:
Our dear Queen Mum has said 'Goodbye'
In London's oldest hall she'll lie
In state, where we can all file past
With prayers and thoughts as our minds cast
Back to other royal days -
When, as a child, my wide-eyed gaze
Fell on another king and queen;
My proud boast is that I have seen
George the Fifth and Queen Mary
Marking their Silver Jubilee.
They drove through streets of London town -
My home was then in Kensington -
With Daddy I had joined the throng
And cheered them as they passed along.
Then, in nineteen thirty-seven,
(I had earlier turned eleven)
Their second son was crowned our king,
For me a most exciting thing;
I heard it on the wireless,
And felt a secret happiness
That I was older than Princess
Elizabeth, our present queen . . .
O what a history I've seen!

Maureen Inglis-Taylor

TABERNACLE WALK (THE EARLY YEARS)

As I think back on early years,
Of happy times and shallow tears,
Recalling hosts of daytime fun,
When summers seemed to have more sun.

Making dens in Grandad's wood,
Playing games we knew we could,
Melted lead in snail shells, cruelish,
Smoking bits of creeper, foolish.

Watch the telly nine inch screen,
Never minding what was seen.
All my friends sat in a row,
Watch the Wilfred Pickles show.

Bows and arrows we did play,
Until that one most dangerous day,
When one got stuck in Gordon's Head,
We all laughed loud, until it bled.
His mother wasn't pleased and so,
Bows and arrows had to go.

We thought we'd have another wheeze,
The parish council we would please,
We set the common well alight,
And then ran off to see the sight.

From behind some trees we looked,
A police car came and we were booked,
The copper read the riot act,
And took us home where we were smacked.
At ten years old it seemed all right,
We'd watched the men set fires alight,
But what we did in early days,
Is now recalled in summer's haze.

John Cook

I WOULDN'T CHANGE A THING

I wouldn't change my childhood for all the tea in China
As childhoods go nothing could be finer
Playing kick the can, we'd amuse ourselves for hours
In the park after dark to borrow your mum some flowers

Climbing trees, bird nesting, catapults and throwing knives
Watch out for the park-keeper better run for your lives
Have you ever run outa breath, but somehow you keep going
Cos if you were caught then your dad would be knowing

We all got up to mischief, never met a kid who ain't
Just trivial things, there again we were no saints
Pushbikes were our transport, sometimes it was shanks
You couldn't take a bike down on the river-banks

Playing football on the green, pitch black, freezing cold
You made your own entertainment and done as you were told
No stealing cars or muggings, picking on the old folk
The old folk once saved England from a German stranglehold

Remember 'Bob a job week', Cubs do jobs for a shilling
Kids don't know they're born today, and they're not as willing
Put a tick in your window so they didn't call twice
We used to help the old folks which was all very nice

Television, mobile phones, computers, it's all laid on a plate
No taxing your brain cos square-eyes is your fate
I wouldn't change anything I did in my childhood
Some folk might disagree, but I think it was very good.

L Smart

SEEMS ONLY YESTERDAY

Well what do you know
Where have you been all these years mate?
Sit yourself down, a coffee or tea?
Meet me wife Kate
Saw your old mum she told me your dad
Still had to work late
Sorry to her your nan died last year
That's hard mate

Seems only yesterday we liked to play
Knockdown ginger
We'd knock at the door of old Missus Moor
She'd come out and say 'Now lads please run away'
Remember the time we all got a fine for speeding
The bobby was right he saved us at night
Speeding's misleading
And old Tommy Ray got tipsy that day on shandy
Not long after that he got his own flat
And married Mandy

Seems only yesterday we liked to play
Knockdown ginger
We'd knock at the door of old Missus Moor
She'd come out and say 'Now lads please run away'
Now I've got two boys and oh what a noise
With their Top of the Pops
And I sometimes feel sad now and know why old dad
Would break out in large spots
But when I look back we've had such a crack
And I'm grateful
For knowing the joy of being a boy
And having me plateful

Seems only yesterday we liked to play
Knockdown ginger.
We'd knock at the door of old Missus Moor
She'd come out and say 'Now lads please run away.'

John Wayre

A BALANCE SHEET OF MEMORIES

We've made great strides in medicine,
And most have much more money.
To sum up times from 'memory lane',
By no means milk and honey.

But then we still have downsides,
Less honesty and care.
Expecting state to underwrite,
And many troubles share.

Our NHS tries to absorb
The mounting need of health.
To win that fight it will require
A greater share of wealth.

If bodily needs are catered for
To extent once thought a dream,
Too many folk with mental ills
Can scarce forbear to scream.

Women have fought for freedom,
Their 'weaker sex' role shed,
Only to gain a burden
Of extra work instead.

Because they are expected
To work out, and at home,
Their children oft are missing out,
Too much inclined to roam.

So, all in all, do we progress?
Are children still our treasure?
We're faced with complex process
For working out that measure.

Don Bishop

GRANDMA'S

Sundays were my favourite.
A visit to Grandma's house is all I needed.

Her pies and home-made lemonade were the best.

Someone whose love was unconditional.
I feel so good inside with her.

I am sure that my mother will
Live up to the role my grandma once did.

Parveen K Saini

DAYS OF YOUTH

What wonderful times spent in a family home
All of sharing and caring together
Living in a country cottage we did not roam
Playing out on the hill whatever the weather

When time was still, extra empty days, slow,
We sent our hoops skimmering with us behind
From the top of a field to the hedge below
Run to the bottom, pick up go on and find

Skipping along the road the usual route
Hopping jumping laughing on our way together
Picking a bunch of wild flowers, sometimes fruit
On the hill above lots and lots of heather

Going out to pick berries on the far moor
Baskets to fill to pick where they abound
A packed lunch tied on as we went out the door
On the hill lovely cold water from the stream underground

In the evenings playing cards, whist, snap, draughts
Making rag rugs to place by our bedside
Walking to the town sometimes, many good laughs
Carefully counting our money used good sense as a guide.

Bessie Groves

THE EIGHTIES - A DECADE OF KALEIDOSCOPIC MEMORIES

On the 2nd of May 81, my mother-in-law passed away,
For all the family and friends, a very sad day.
On the 26th of May 81, my youngest daughter was born,
Joy unbounded though our hearts were still torn.

In 82, the Falklands war with Argentina erupted,
People wondering how and why our lives were interrupted.
In 83, Maggie Thatcher threatened the miners,
An overtime ban to weaken and undermine us.

March 84 saw the miners strike start,
Fighting for fair conditions, much searching of heart.
A year long struggle for equality and justice,
Twelve months deprivation and government prejudice.

March 85 saw a triumphant return to employment,
Much restructuring and rebuilding without enjoyment.
85 also saw my first marriage failing,
Although it must be said without too much wailing.

87 was when the divorce papers were served,
She got much more than she really deserved.
89 was the year I again heard wedding bells,
And embarked on truly the marriage from hell.

So there you have a ten-year slice of my life,
The highs and the lows, the joy and the strife.
These are the things that alter and shape us,
Hopefully without too much pain or fuss.

David Muncaster

A VILLAGE SUMMER

Summer mornings drenched with dew,
Skylarks hovering, blackbirds singing.
Rippling stream like sparkling diamonds,
This was our village in summer.

A reaper cutting through the hay,
Spreading a perfume like no other.
Rabbits fleeing, farmers shooting,
This was summer as we knew it.

This was summer in the village,
Summer dresses made of voile.
Straw hats, white gloves, and canvas shoes,
Pristine white, cleaned with 'Blanco'.

Garden fêtes and sales of work,
Bran tubs, raffles, and ice cream.
Who would win the pig this year?
We all waited breathlessly.

Cricket matches on the green,
Wives and mothers serving teas.
Men in white, so very smart,
A draw will put us all at ease.

Church bells ringing on Sunday morning,
Off to church in our Sunday best.
To attend the morning service,
Home to lunch, feeling blest.

Summertime in our village,
Holds such memories for me.
Happy days, sunny days,
But to stay was not to be.

Mabel Barber

YESTERDAY

I only have to set eyes on you
And that's good enough for me
The overcliff's winding path
Leading down towards the sea
Sunlight shimmering onto a turquoise surface
Waves racing towards the shore
It's wonderful to journey back
To this place once more
Golden expanses of sand
Stretching as far as the eye can see
Past reminders - so heavenly
I can't but help daydreaming
Whilst I simply stare
What became of the child upon that beach
Now but a shadow with golden hair

Katherine Parker

DOWN MEMORY LANE

As I go back down memory lane
Through all those years - what did I gain?
Not fame nor fortune was my lot
But what a wonderful family I've got.
This I've gathered along life's way
Like beautiful flowers on a summer's day.
They are my treasures - that I now own
And never do I feel alone.
Children, grandchildren all around
With their love and affection I abound.
So precious treasures of mine
I'll love you till the end of time.

John Townend

THOUGHTS FROM MEMORY LANE

I sit alone, in a beautiful home,
Thinking of past years -
With family love and friends of yore
How could anyone ask for more?

Now times have changed, and life has too -
Yet love remains the same.
With children around to cuddle and hold,
I find it by far, more precious than gold.

A knock on the door, a youth stood there,
'Can't pass without calling, Nan dear' . . .
A feeling of bliss, a goodnight kiss -
Keeps holding back the years.

Oh, yes, I am rich, with memories dear,
A loving family ever near,
Feel warmth within, so I'll not give in,
I'll lift up my chin! - when troubles appear!

Ivy Cawood

WHATEVER HAPPENED TO VIMTO?

Whatever happened to Vimto
The amber coloured nectar glugged down greedily on the way home from school?
And Spanish Root sucked till its juices ran dry?
What could compete with Ovaltine tablets the staple diet chewed non-stop
At the Saturday matinee in the cinema
While sitting in rapture at the antics of the Three Stooges
Or if you were really lucky Superman . . . to be continued next week
Was it really only a shilling for a ticket?
The magic of the wireless, hearing adults laughing at Tommy Handley
And Ted Ray
Not knowing why they were laughing, but joining in the laughter anyway
The heady delights of Monday night at eight, and
The Adventures of Dick Barton, Special Agent
The eagerly anticipated weekly trip to the library
Hooked on the literary goddesses of Blyton, and Brazil
Reading with the torch beneath the bed clothes after lights out
Secure in the knowledge you were defying your parents
Simple pleasures that would mainly be derided now
Whatever happened to childhood?

Adrianne Jones

CHILDHOOD MEMORIES

I remember as if it was yesterday
the most precious days of my life, I would say.
A special time spent, with no worries or stress
just which toys to play with; which buttons to press?

Those games that we played filled us with such glee
like jumping the yogga, just Salvie and me.
We'd slide down the stairs (head first), with a thump
as we landed below, oh dear, what a bump!

My first day at school was quite an event
those tears, how they flowed, no one could invent.
The anguish and fear, I could not pretend
but soon all was fine, thanks to a new friend.

The fights that we had, I remember them well
for dear Mum and Dad, it must have been yell.
But soon battles done, they never did last
all three, now good friends, the storm cloud had passed.

Those memories we have will always be there
that big sis' and I do so often share.
No one can replace the times now gone by
such special kept thoughts that will never die.

Claudia Colella

MEMORIES ARE MADE OF THIS

I've known you since you were aged twenty-one
A beautiful bride, the sun shone on.
Many years have gone since then
For a while it was just Viv and Ken
Then Michelle arrived upon the scene
The loveliest daughter ever seen
Family complete with arrival of Paul
Two proud parents walking so tall.
The memory I will always remember
Was Christmas days 25th December
A thoughtful neighbour, you fetched me
To watch the children take gifts from the tree
The biggest blow that broke my heart
You were leaving for Devon, we were to part
Time has passed and we're still friends
If the Lord doesn't come he always sends
There's letters, and phone calls, and visits to me
Whenever you're here in Coventry.
Michelle and Paul at universities passed
Both now working, long may it last
You're fifty this year, Viv and Ken
The reason, I've picked up my pen
Was so that I could write and say
Loving wishes, happy birthday.

Joan Jeffries

HOLIDAYS WITH GRANDMA

On holidays of childhood memory's sun will always shine
On hours of carefree happiness. Such memories are mine.
We did not ask for luxuries; we thrived on simple fare,
With appetites well sharpened by the wholesome country air.
Our milk came straight from milkman's churn, eggs from the man
                                                                                 next-door,
Ripe gooseberries, lettuce, carrots from the long back garden's store,
No bottled squash or fizzy drinks. For lack of these who'd care?
Cold water from the garden pump was drink beyond compare.
In theme park fields a bird's nest or a grass snake might be found.
The see-saw by the garden fence supplied our pleasure ground.
With pimpernel for weather vane and dandelions for clocks
We'd deck ourselves with daisy chains, rub nettle stings with docks.
Outside the tiny sweet shop, penny clutched, we'd peer within
At bulls' eyes, peardrops, sherbet dabs, the choice could then begin.
Familiar was the grocery store, its paraffin and rope,
Dim lighting and the mingled smells of bacon, cheese and soap.
At tea-time, seated on the grass, we'd eat thick buttered bread
With Grandma's home-made mixed fruit jam so generously spread.
An evening walk down high-hedged lanes till sun began to sink,
Then into that soft feather bed, asleep without a blink.

V E Godfrey

THE FIELD DAY - 1937

Beneath an azure August sky
A Sunday School, with banner high
Wound its way from dingy street
Led by a band with a martial beat
Resplendent in their caps and braid
Proud as guardsmen on parade.

A stubble field reached at last
And with excitement rising fast
The children ran to rows of stalls
Oblivious to the teachers' calls
And with voices, some with lisps
Purchased minerals, ices, crisps.

Little girls in gingham dresses
Plaited pigtails, beribboned tresses,
Little boys in shirt and shorts
Keen to test their friends at sports,
A coloured cloud of butterflies
Swirling around with eager eyes.

They entered in the various races
Showing their athletic paces,
Be it sack or egg and spoon,
Three-leg or blow a balloon
For each winner a handsome prize
And rousing cheers for the good tries.

Where are they now, children of yore?
The older ones soon called to war
And history has turned the page
On that different time, that bygone age
And the tradition of the annual fête
Is yet another forgotten date.

Robert E Fraser

DREAMS DON'T LAST FOREVER

Dreams don't last forever
Thoughts must be returned
If time should stop in December,
Will the sun cease to burn?

People must give together
The love that they possess
For life on Earth is temporary,
From the moment of your birth.

Though Heaven and Hell are in me
I fail to understand
If dreams don't last forever
What then, is the purpose of man?

There may be no reason
To be or to die alone
Yet I am sure of the season,
Now the autumn leaves have gone!

Brendan G Ryan

THOSE WERE THE DAYS

Remember the days of dip-in pens,
Pink blotting paper, the old inkwell?
How much work had you done on that day?
With one look at your hands you could tell.

Given the job of ink monitor,
The instructions rang out loud and clear,
'Just fill them all right up to the top,
Be careful not to spill any dear.'

Now this was easier said than done,
Many desks were wet, shiny and blue.
So when you tried to blot it all up
The size of the pool just grew and grew.

Trying to draw lines with a ruler,
It moved, the ink splodged all down the page.
Testing even for the best in class,
Calmest pupils flew into a rage.

Every day seemed to pose a challenge,
Nibs broke, so into the bin you'd fling!
Who needed dip-in pens anymore?
With new fountain pen you were 'class king'.

Angela Pritchard

A Memory To Cherish

Those distant days with happy ways, of simply having fun.
Of sandwiches and lemonade and faces in the sun.
At Sunday school they had a rule so plain, it said 'No shouting'.
Ignore it at your peril or for you, no church day outing.

To see those happy faces all sitting neat in rows.
The driver turns the engine on and waving, off she goes.
We're going on our outing, the sun is way up high
And polka dots for tiny clouds are floating in the sky.

The bus slows down we all get off and stand in line like guards.
The teacher gives us all our names wrote down on bits of cards.
At half past three you look for me and here I will be found.
I won't have time if you don't come to stop and look around.

The constant nudging all around and then we all make way.
Into the park to play our games and laugh away the day.
First the egg and spoon race then jumping in the sack.
When out of breath I almost won, but landed on my back.

Next came out the rounders, we had to beat the girls.
We threw the ball so very fast towards the one with curls.
She never even bothered to hit the ball, you see.
But then she went and hit it hard, right past the boundary.

And there we were our faces red but not from off the sun.
The girls had done it once again and shouted 'We have won.'
Sad but not down hearted played cricket what a score.
The vicar who with one swipe struck out and scored a four.

The thrill of just competing was shown on every face
And never really caring if you won or lost the race.
That day will last forever, fixed tight with super glue.
Upon my heart it played a part, I'm sure it does for you.

R E Weedall

NOSTALGIA

Polished and pampered you had such appeal
As your driver climbed in took his place at the wheel.
A turn of the key and you came so alive
And always seemed eager to go for a drive,
You made us feel special, you fulfilled our dreams
The sights of the country, of rivers and streams,
You gave us such joy and such pleasure each day.
As far from the city we'd go on our way,
You'd drink your life's blood at a stop that we made,
The engine was checked and the bill duly paid.
We'd go out on the highway as free as a bird,
You made other vehicles look quite absurd.
The brag of a Jag, the scold of a Rolls, the Minx as she slinked
                                                                       by your side,
By such as a Ford you were thoroughly bored
But you had to take note when the copper's car called!
Body so dumpy, we travelled so far
In our fabulous, favourite, first Mini car.

Jan Edmunds

SUNDAYS

We'd go to the church dressed in our Sunday best
Where we would say prayers so that we could be blessed.
We all walked sedately with prayer books in hand,
Arriving there early - those late had to stand.
The vicar would tell us we had to rejoice
So I'd sing the hymns at the top of my voice.

While mentally noting the people not there,
The whole congregation would kneel down in prayer
Then after the service, in groups they would chat
And tittle and tattle about this and that
While all of the children stood quiet and neat
And hoped to eat muffins for their Sunday treat.

We slowly walked home taking care not to scratch
Our nice shiny shoes which our outfits would match.
Once home, it was boring, we just had to sit
We weren't allowed sewing or even to knit,
But told 'Read the Bible to learn about God'
And to disobey meant a stroke from the rod!

At teatime the table was laid with great care
With all the best china and real silverware.
We had to watch manners and always said grace
Then when we had finished we stayed in our place
Till all of the family had eaten their fill
Then we thanked the Lord who had shown his goodwill.

Joy Saunders

BLACKBERRYING 1999

Down the lane the blackberries grew,
And in September when the dew
Was on the grass, where grazed the sheep,
Mushrooms would pop up while you sleep;
For every country child would know
Where there are sheep mushrooms grow.

And when at noon the sun was high,
And in the fields the grass was dry,
Hedges were thick with brambles where
The scent of ripe fruit filled the air.
Then armed with baskets and a stick
We'd choose our patch and start to pick.

But teasing nature aims to teach,
So sets the best just out of reach,
To gain her prize we'd need our stick
To hook the brambles laden thick
With all the ripest fruit, to fill
Each his own small basket, till
Hungry, tired, and juicy red
We'd turn for home, and tea and bed.

All this I knew - and lived again
When recently I found a lane
That had escaped the slasher's tear,
And there were blackberries everywhere!
Then, as I gathered nature's store
I was a little girl once more.

Joyce Preddle

DAYS GONE BY

When we are young we don't think of getting old,
We play with our friends and do as we are told,
Our school days were the best and it put us to the test,
To prepare for the future wherever it may rest.
The laughter and the fun we had when we were young

We would go to the playground and get upon the swings
And up and down the chute we'd go then on the roundabout
And have a game of football and maybe cricket too
Don't forget the rounders a game we'll have no doubt

A trip to see our granny and dear old grandad too
A tin of broken biscuits which makes us a bit 'fu'
Off we would pop to the sweetie shop for a penny caramel
And I wouldn't share mine I would eat it all ma'sel
And back up to Granny's to ring her new doorbell

Now it's getting late and we'll be heading out the gate
Back home to our beds we're very tiring 'nough' said
Supper then lights out, when we were young
That's what it was all about.

Joseph Broadley

MISSING YOU

I cherish all the happy times
We shared together
Memories of you
Of the things we did
We often look at the photos
Of you, me and the kids
I'm sure that God took you
To ease all your pain
And he will keep you safe
Until we meet again

G Morrisey

THE LITTLE HOUSE

Little house, it seems but yesterday, your door stood open wide,
To welcome me, as eagerly I came and stepped inside.
Little house, it seems but yesterday, with husband at my side,
I dwelt beneath your friendly roof, a carefree, youthful bride.

Little house, it seems but yesterday, within your sheltering care,
I cradled my dear firstborn child, a tiny girl so fair.
Little house, it seems but yesterday, when children romped at play,
A healthy growing family, safe in your walls each day.

Little house, it seems but yesterday, as joy and sorrow came,
We knew the blessing of this home, unchanging, still the same.
Little house, if only walls could talk, what stories you would tell!
The ups and downs of family life, you knew each member well.

Little house, those yesterdays have gone, the children have all grown.
As adults now, just like the birds, each one the nest has flown!
Little house, alas, the time has come for me to bid farewell,
And sadly now, I have to break from your enchanted spell.

Little house, ah, when tomorrow comes and I from you have gone,
A part of me will still remain, although I have moved on.
Little house, as you in future years make others welcome too,
Fond memories will come to me, when I remember you.

Eileen Phillis

A Thought Of You

Just a little thought of you as I sit here in my chair,
I often think of past times, you are often there.
As you were in childish years in amongst my hopes and fears.
Here today remembering many memories I hold
Of us and years together, in the family fold.
Those events and occasions we had within our clan
With sons and daughters from this woman and this man.
Of memories of our family this is a special day
The last day all together, they do not fade, just tucked away.
This time of year we all recall the days that used to be
You and I and other members of our family.
I hope you are well at your work and play
With the life you have chosen, many would envy you today.
I like to think you are 'comfy' in your daily life,
Ignore the media news, so much conflict, so much strife.
Loving considerations in far distance separations,
Just another thought of you as years go by with speed,
You understood all my childish needs.
Be happy in surroundings where I picture you,
Have faith and trust in God, in everything you do.

P Evans

WHITSUN TREAT

We always rose early on that special day
Hoping the weather would be sunny,
Down to the village green we would go -
Bags packed, shoes cleaned, clutching our precious money.
Up on to the lorries, with slatted-wood chairs
We would sit and wave goodbye,
Singing and laughing as we rode along
Sunday School banners waving high.
The farmer's field held many adventures
With cricket and rounders to play,
Jam buns, fruit cake and a mug of tea
Was our lunch at twelve mid-day.
There was always ice cream and raspberryade
Toffee apples and barley sugar sweets
A bygone age of wonderful days -
The Sunday School Whitsun Treats.

Jean F Mackenzie

CHRISTMAS PAST

What do you want for Christmas,
now you're all grown up?

It seems there's nothing left to do
but stand on by, and look
At all the toys, books and games
that fill the shops and stores.

Waiting for collection from
good old Santa Claus
Who used to call at our house
when you were very small.

With baby dolls, prams and books,
soaps and chocolate treats
A hundred different parcels
in the corner, at your feet.

The magic filled the winter night
straight to bed with eyes closed tight
To dream your dreams of Santa's sleigh,
across the skies, he's on his way.

A mince pie for his reindeer,
a glass of port for him,
The footprints in the morning snow
that told you he had been.

So what's happened to old Santa?
I miss him now, don't you?
Remembering those special times
he brought for me and you.

I guess it comes from growing up,
we seem not to have the time,
For simple thoughts of make believe,
that we have left behind.

But maybe if we can pretend
that we are young again
Then all that magic will return
and he might call again.

S P Johnson

MEMORIES OF GRAN

Memories of far-off days
Come flooding back to me,
Certain smells remove the haze
And the years fall away instantly.

I'm in my grandma's bed once more
At the smell of candle grease
With white-washed ceiling, big oak door,
Flock mattress and pillow I lie in peace.

To smell sizzling bacon on the stove
I close my eyes and see
The dear old lady I dearly loved,
She meant all the world to me.

But now she's gone, and I have wept
She rests now in God's keeping.
Winter, summer, she has slept
The sleep that's everlasting.

Valerie McKinley

STEP BACK IN TIME

I long to turn back the hands of the clock,
and go back to my childhood day,
to wander lush meadows, now long since gone,
visit the milly where we used to play.

We fished in the babbling brook with our nets,
took tadpoles we caught, home in a jar,
now a four lane motorway replaces that spot,
a noisy, festering and hideous scar.

I yearn to go back to my childhood haunts,
to the woods where the bluebells grew,
and the primroses flourished so abundantly,
where the sweet scented breezes blew,
we watched rabbits at play, if we kept very still,
saw the skylark flying heavenwards singing,
chased the Camberwell beauty as it fluttered by,
felt the peace all around us gently clinging.

I yearn for that peace and tranquillity now,
when all strangers soon became friends,
but so much has changed, it's no good looking back,
our old ways are replaced by modern trends.

Pamela Eckhardt

HANDSTANDS

Standing on my hands
Feet firm against the wall
The next one has to land
Wait till you hear her call
All our legs and hands neatly in a line
Strange shapes, our shadows cast

One, two, three, four, five
Me, Mary, Janet and Jane, Maria always last

Practise makes perfect
Hope we do not fall
One eye out for the Prefect
Or detention after school
Children gather around us
Amazed at our trick

Me, Mary, Janet, Jane, Maria always last
Has the final kick

Like a team of gymnastics
Going for the gold
Upright like a ship's mast
Ooops! I'm losing hold
Down we tumble, one and all
I think we need a nurse

Me, Mary, Janet and Jane
This time Maria first.

Linda Doel

BACK TO THEN

Lay back, arms raised, hands cushioning your head
Look up, see the blue of the sky and the puffy white clouds
Smell that salty tang and feel that warmth seeping into your skin
Take a deep breath, then . . . let it all begin.

Close your eyes, drift away, float into that time between
You can hear the gentle wash of the waves being sieved through
The pebbles, you can feel the hardness of the stones pressing into
                                                                                           your spine
Go on, think right back . . . to your childhood time.

Days of freedom, grab a towel, cycle up the road to the beach
Those days you couldn't feel the shingle under your feet
You just ran down straight into the sea, laughing, splashing having fun
Wonderful days . . . life just begun.

Then the other days when the weather had turned again
The wind blowing blustery, seagulls winging over white
                                                                                     whipped waves
You stood on the wall watching, your hair streaming back, tears falling
Somehow sad but also glad . . . and teatime calling.

Come back to now with your eyes squinting, a whiteness all around
The sun reflecting off the mirror-still sea, a speedboat droning by,
                                                                                      water frothing,
Children screaming, laughing, now the smell of picnic lunches and fish
'Oh well!' you sigh, 'all is normal' . . . but don't you wish.

Elizabeth Martin

EARLY DAYS AT SCHOOL

I have a little photo of my infant class at school,
I've treasured it for years, though it's now the worse for wear.
It brings back many memories, both glad and not so good
For I hated school when first I went, but later all that changed.
After I got over the first initial shock, I came to like my schooldays
And began to read and write, instead of sorting coloured wools
And make paper lanterns with a handle at the top
Out of flowered wallpaper we had to bring from home.
Or learning how to draw a horse, a dog or cows and sheep.
That was only kids' stuff, but to read and write was clever,
The sort of thing that grown-ups did with pen and ink and paper.
We also learned to count on an abacus with balls.
They have machines to do it now, but then it was more fun.
The school was built of red brick with a playground at the front
Where pandemonium reigned whenever school came out to play.
The teacher blew a whistle when we had to go back in.
Sometimes I saw my grandma at the entrance gates.
She used to call me over to get a special treat,
An apple, a banana or a handful of boiled sweets.
My mother told her that was wrong.
She should not give me things.
She said I'd never settle if she kept on doing that.
When I see the smiling faces in the battered photograph
They make these memories flood back, and I am young again.
Standing in assembly to celebrate the Empire,
To wave a union flag and sing Jerusalem,
The moving words of Parry's famous song.

Kathleen McGowan

ONCE UPON A TIME

So many memories of days that used to be,
So many thoughts of things when we were young and free.
No electronic games to steal our precious time.
No television soaps or tales of Yankie crime.
We had our own wondrous world of games for to play,
Thoughts of which make me still tingle even today.
Coccarooso! Mountie Kitty! and Kick the Tin!
Hoist The Flag! Delivo! Cannon! and Three Goes In!
These were all our street games played with an endless zest,
To bring us a happy childhood, they were the best.
Come, let us have some sympathy for the kids now,
Burdened down with the burgers filled with dodgy cow,
While static behind the computer flashing screens.
Surely we have got the gumption and the very means,
To take our youngsters down far more worthy pathways,
So they can look back to their own fulfilled young days.

William Hunt-Vincent

EARLY DAYS

We whiled away the hours playing football in the park
The time it passed so quickly we ended in the dark
We often played with teams of twelve and sometimes even more
The results just didn't matter though there was often a disputed score.

We sometimes played a game of tennis especially in June
We had to pay for that and the endings were all too soon
The park-keeper would blow his whistle and tell us 'Time to go!'
We would leave the court and play on the grass till the light
                                                                     was much too low

Cricket in the street with the lamppost as the wicket
Passed many a summer night, it was just the ticket
With so few cars to distract us the game went on and on
It gave us all plenty of time to score an eventual ton

On Sunday mornings out would come my trusty pedal bike
I would cycle for hours going anywhere I like
I'd cycle to school a few miles away every weekday morning
But when it rained, I used the bus, which was very boring

Each Saturday morning we would go to the local baths for a swim
We would be there for eight o'clock and stay in there until ten
But in the afternoon, it was time for the big game
West Bromwich Albion, or Walsall, the pleasure was the same

So I look back and wonder on how it came to be
That I had so little time that I could say was free
You hear so many kids today 'There's nothing for me to do,'
I must have been so lucky, I guess I am one of the few.

Mike Fisher

Memories

I'm sitting in my armchair
Relaxed without a care.
I'm thinking of my childhood
When I went everywhere.
I've scaled some quite high mountains
I've sailed upon the seas
I've travelled on the airways
And always been at ease.
The time sped by so quickly
The years just slipped away
Till I woke up one morning
And realised my hair was grey.
As I gazed thereon in horror
I saw with great dismay
The wrinkles on my forehead
Just wouldn't go away.
My heart felt full of longing
For the days of long ago
Yet still I have my memories
To make my heart just glow.
I'm really very grateful
My life was great you know.

D Adams

LIFE'S EXCURSION

Here begins life's long excursion - memories past that we can build on,
I oft-times stroll down memory lane - some past events to view again,
Like outings to a sandy shore - with Sunday School each year we'd go,
Excited then were all of us - at hill-stop waiting for our bus.
Ice cream cart - 'stop me and buy one' all well planned for our excursion
And *ages* later, shouts of glee - from first to see the deep blue sea.
Out came bathers, buckets and spades - on water's edge the
                                                                                youngest wades.
Some older more adventurous braves - with running jump would ride
                                                                                 the waves!
Then after all the games and fun - we'd towel dry and dress in sun,
Then sitting round in one large ring - our songs from Sunday School
                                                                                we'd sing,
And other times from Bluebell Wood, we'd take to mother, a big load
Not every time met with good grace - 'Where shall I put them?' said
                                                                                her face,
But mother, being always kind - would soon a special corner find,
And whinberry picking by the ton - or so it seemed when we
                                                                               were young
So often they'd spill on the floor - and mountain top we'd climb
                                                                                 for more.
In those days, we were safe and sound 'tho far we'd wander from
                                                                            home ground.
These happy thoughts and many more - are for recall in memory's store.
Remembered times we oft can share - with friends and others who
                                                                               were there.
Age now has halted days of play, but these thoughts keep old age at bay
And we look forward when day's done to years long in life's excursion.

Marian Curtis-Jones

DOWN MEMORY LANE

We walked across the fields to school,
We looked for tadpoles in the pools;
We picked some flowers to cheer up Gran,
If bull in field we sometimes ran.

At school in desks we always sat,
No walking round or simple chat;
Our tables learnt by heart each day,
A weekly poem we had to say.

When home from school we did our chores,
We cleaned the shoes and went to stores;
We tended gardens, small but neat,
We kept a pig for meat to eat.

We learnt to milk the cows by hand,
We did some work upon the land;
At hoeing time our backs did ache,
At harvest time the fields we rake.

To Sunday school each week we went,
For any gift a note was sent;
When someone came to visit house,
We sat in room like silent mouse.

We sat together for dinner and tea,
No one dare move till plate was free;
On Sunday nights we walked or rode,
The family always followed code.

On savings card our stamps we placed,
When time for play, to field we raced;
We loved our parents throughout each day,
Each night we knelt, our prayers to say.

John Paulley

CHANGING YEARS

Buttercups glowing yellow under my chin!
Small, white daisies joined by stalks so thin!
My throat beautified by this gift from green slopes.
With my childlike dreams and my childlike hopes!

Aniseed balls in triangular packets.
Hockey sticks and tennis rackets.
Bread and dripping for breakfast, instead of jam.
Sunday's luxury of leg of lamb!

Clip-clopping down the street in Mother's shoes.
Kennedy and Kruschev filled the news!
Pressed flowers in books to preserve their beauty.
Conscripted soldiers do their duty!

Endless net petticoats like crinoline times.
Fluorescent socks replace nursery rhymes.
Embroidered tablecloths for the bottom drawer.
The wedding dress that Mother wore!

Busy roads have bubble cars with lift-up roofs.
Taking the place of horses' hooves.
Juke boxes and cola, we patiently sit.
Awaiting to hear Cliff's latest hit!

Hair back-combed so high it looked like a hive.
A waltz transforming into the jive!
Stiletto heels get jammed into pavement cracks.
Journeys to my love down railway tracks!

Holding open car doors to allow me inside.
Respect and courtesy always the guide.
Those days have long gone with the passing of years.
The happy faces exchanged for tears!

Val Spall

Memory

No one knows quite how I feel,
So lonely and so sad,
Give my heart some time to heal,
It won't be quite so bad.

I recollect the vast white sands,
The time I spent with you,
I cover my face up with my hands,
I'm feeling rather blue.

I go to sleep, but in my dreams,
I am with you again,
I feel alive, my face it beams,
But when I wake, it's pain.

I stare into the cloudy sky,
And remember happily,
The best time of my entire life,
Was it not meant to be?

I telephone your mobile phone,
I need to hear your voice,
I wish that it was not this way,
But do I have a choice?

Although it hurts inside my soul,
When my heart was slain,
It brought about that deep black hole,
Where this memory shall remain.

Katy Sturman

UNTITLED

I remember those walks of long ago
For a walk I take it slow.
But the world has changed that for me,
I just can't go one my own anymore
I would not feel safe you see
But it was so peaceful for me
There were blackberries to pick.
We'd take our tea my friend and me.
My son sometimes he would say
'Mother we will take the dogs today.'
Now it's no longer safe for me:
Why should this have to be?
God gave us the world to share
Why should I be frightened to go there?

Roma Skrzypczak

OLD FRIENDS

Step back in time with me my friend
Step back in time with me
There's the field where once I played
And this my favourite tree.
Through fallen leaves we'd kick our way
Let's do it once just now,
Played games in the old school yard
Come let me show you how.
Remember German measles?
You caught that from me,
We skipped, we ran and shouted
Fell and grazed a knee.
We had a gang, we had a den
Built high up in a tree
The old familiar voice of Mother
Called us for our tea.
Step back in time with me my friend
Wander memory lane
Whatever things I used to do
I guess you did the same.

Colin Boynton

THOSE HAPPY DAYS

I remember those happy days,
The limited company that was you and me,
Our late night politics and silly ways,
Laughing, loving and feeling free.

Sharing secrets, jokes and passions,
Singing songs, not worrying 'bout the tune
Our alternative music and careless fashions,
Talking till dawn and waking at noon.

School days were almost bearable because of you,
Having my best friend by my side,
Knowing it would always be me and Lou,
Not having to worry if I cried.

I miss the love, laughter and being free,
Miss the talking, sleepovers and ridiculous den,
I miss our limited company,
Sometimes wish it was still then.

Kate Strutt

A SIGN OF THE TIMES

Once long ago on a day just like today,
   people talked and went for walks to pass the time away.
Children walked to school alone,
   the thought of danger wasn't known.

When cars were a luxury and owned by few,
   and it didn't matter that nothing was new.
Football in the road, your father might play,
   things that were urgent were done the next day.

The policeman patrolled all day on his bike,
   order he kept by day and night.
Of muggings and rape we heard not a word,
   bad language a thing we never much heard.

Schooldays were happy days, or so I was told,
   the winters were miserable and cold, oh, so cold.
I quite like to look back on those halcyon days,
   they were the best in so many ways.

Colin Spicer

FROM TIME TO TIME

Sometimes I wander once again
Down what we used to call 'Our Lane'.
In spring bluebells can still be found,
In autumn mushrooms hug the ground.
In early year the birds are nesting,
Feeding fledglings, never resting,
And later, when the acorns show,
Squirrels bustle to and fro
Gathering stores to hide away
For a later, hungrier day.
Some days a sea mist creeping in
Hangs silver threads where spiders spin,
Or frost decks all with sparkling lace,
Or snow creates a magic place,
And on such quiet, mystic days,
As light among the shadows plays,
Along the path I seem to see
A small, grey dog waiting for me,
But as I near he fades from sight -
A figment of mind? A trick of light?
Or, in a time-warp, a re-play
Of moments from a bygone day?

M U Stein

LOOKING BACK

As I approach my fiftieth year,
Life is good and the road ahead clear.
When I think back, and I do often now,
To a time that was innocent and slower somehow.
Being a child of the fifties not long after the war,
Sweets were still rationed and the rent man came to the door.
Growing up was really great fun,
Long summer days and lots of sunburn.
Playing all day as cowboys with guns,
Being told to come in before the last blink of sun.
Never any worries, never any fears
But things started to change in the teenage years.
A real know it all, who couldn't be told
What do you know, you're really old.
But as the years roll by, quite faster than you know
The real understanding doesn't come as such a blow.
I look forward now, not to the Old Age Pension
Rather to fulfilling some dreams and retirement with a long extension.

Charles Trail

LOST YEARS

What happened to those middle years
Inextricably engulfed by hopes and fears?
They seemed to limp by traumatically
As one coped with life, automatically.

Days melted by immersed in family life,
Avoiding, if possible, both storm and strife;
Trying to encourage, soothe and care,
Covering emotions when they were laid bare.

And now one is left, wondering how
There is this gap between then and now.
As life's span is diminishing fast,
A need is born to delve into the past.

Happiness remains elusive and rare,
I never expected life to be fair.
I search for meaning and fulfilment,
For shared hopes and contentment.

Why are those middle years so elusive?
Why are struggle and sadness so obtrusive?
I must look deeper for meaning and fun,
The long search for truth has just begun!

S J Dodwell

DAY TRIPS

As I wander this lonely shore,
Thoughts and memories do haunt me more.
I feel a stirring in my heart, and then the tears begin to start,
And these will go on for a while,
But parts of my memory will make me smile.
Familiar thoughts then enter my mind,
I hear the laughter of every child.
Their screams of delight as they jump into the sea,
What wonderful days they used to be.
We stroll on the prom,
Perhaps buy a little gift for family and friends.
We wish these days would never end,
But they do, and it's time to go home.
And over the years the children grow up,
And soon have a life of their own.
Then my memory grows dim and I'm back on the shore,
I look at the beach and walk some more.
The sand stretching out,
Never-ending it seems,
And the rocks rising high, almost touching the sky.
The melancholy cry of the gulls as they come in to land.
Not another sound to be heard,
Just the breaking of waves on the sand,
This place is deserted this time of the year,
All the shops boarded up and just standing bare.
But memories my darling can still make me smile,
If I just sit down and dream for a while.

Tom Usher

My Memories

Close my eyes and then I listen to the sound of music;
The beat of the fairground music of years long ago,
There is goes all over again taking me back to my childhood;
Remembering days and years half a century ago,

I stand transfixed for a moment by the crumbling buildings;
Gone are the pavements and I see horses and carts I know,
It must be May for the horses have silks on their manes;
The carts they are pulling have fairy lights all aglow,

Men with rolling cigarettes and cloth caps are passing,
Girls from factories and mills on their homeward way are bound,
The fairground lights are now all twinkling,
I watch dobby horses going round and round,

Men, women and children into a tent are hurrying,
They eat black peas uttering not a sound,
On wooden benches the men and women are closely sitting,
Children are crossed legged on the straw strewn ground,

I come out of this trance finding yellow cabs rushing by
Sounds are louder with scenes frightening to my eye
I am amazed at the buildings with windowed lifts
Shoppers ascending and descending holding gifts,

The boys and girls wearing denim with pony tails,
My guess at their sexes now always fails.
At the top of the Empire State Building I look around,
Amazed at the hundreds of lights all around,

On the grey line buses upstairs I go
I look at the stores with their goods on show.
The foods on display are all new to me
Coming from countries I read about in geography,

From the open top buses I view upper New York
And later on I view down town New York
Yes, times have changed for the better, I pray
It is the twentieth century in New York USA.

I Foxcroft

FIRST MEETING

In time gone by my memory says,
A voice I heard and my heart was pleased,
Its lilting sound and those soft words,
Like a flow of music that I did need.
Her gentle smile and light soft touch,
As down that moonlit road we speed.
We ride on, neither asked for much,
Scenery changed without a touch.

Yet time stood still within our sphere.
People passed as shadows deep,
And nothing we ourselves did hear.
Stops and starts repeatedly,
One boarded others went,
Yet being together was our desire.
Until we reached our journey's end.

We knew that now we'd have to part.
To meet again as our intent,
Our relationship to which we had made a start.
Ensured our life would alter now,
As we kept in touch by word and speech.
Letters written with words so dear,
Those that no one else could hear,
To build on friendship true.

Kenneth Copley

THE SHAMBLES

Up and down cottages, row upon row,
Gardens covered in weeds and brambles
Would have been occupied a long time ago.
Neglected area named 'The Shambles'.

Imagine families worked or drew 'the dole'
In those depressive times,
Dads and lads went down the hole,
Dawn to dusk in company mines.

Women worked to better their lot,
Could work for a time through the day
A shilling or two is all they got,
Not much to show for their pay.

Children were cheery little souls,
Played games with not much learning,
Climbed the slack heap, scraping coals,
To keep the home fires burning.

Community spirit brought blessings but few,
Neighbourly love and support.
In every cottage one another they knew
Though scraps and battles were fought.

No more sounds now the dwellings are dead,
No thoughts, or even contrition.
No feelings or words or anything said.
The Shambles are facing demolition.

Bernice Sharpe

REFLECTIONS

A slow walk along a leafy lane
The sound of gentle showery rain
And then a house comes into view
Black leaden roof and walls of blue.

The garden pond where weeds grow high
The babbling crystal stream nearby
The meadow where we loved to run
A reminder of days filled with fun.

We'd clamber up the rocky hill
And for a while time stood still
Then down again we all would race
Each one eager for first place.

Behind the house the shed stands bare
Keeping secrets once shared there
The yard lies still, remembering
Children's laughter in early spring.

I remember so well the games we would play
Just as if it were yesterday
And even though many years have passed
These memories will always last.

Now all that's left is an empty space
But I know time cannot replace
All that's happened here before
As I turn around and shut the door.

Stephanie Henley

WAR EFFORT

In the drear, dear days of yore,
before TV, still pre-victorious,
as future pillars of our glorious nation,
we of the wartime generation -

pigeon-toed, plookie, peelie-wally,
scrofulous and undernourished,
knock-kneed, halitosic, mousy,
chilpit, rickety and lousy -

to prevent TB got school milk free,
and consequently flourished.
Each week was bleakly, boringly foreseeable -
hence disagreeable.

Day 1: for fatties, mince 'n' tatties.
Day 2: a sort of Irish stew.
Day 3: ah, me. We sought relief
      in cabbage, mash and corned beef.
Day 4: (There's more.) Toad-in-the-hole
      squatting obscenely in the bowl.
      (None of us ever known to beg
      for more reconstituted egg.)
Day 5: To stay alive, o look! An ashet,
      dash it, bearing snoek.
      (Our mum, thank God, was quite unable
      to finagle whalemeat to the table).
Day 6: (I reminisce with pain) - was back to corned beef again.
Day 7: Invariably, spam 'n' pickles.
      Still, here I am. I laugh. It tickles.

Through sacrifice, we crushed the Hun,
conquered the Bosch. Their days were done.
Then, early in 1947, my first banana. Oh,what heaven!

Norman Bissett

JUST DREAMING

The baker's shop was open on time,
People waiting in a long line,
Once a year,
That special Friday was here,
Hot cross buns, by the bagful,
Children waiting for a mouthful.

Hot cross buns, hot cross buns,
The skipping ropes were turning,
Children out skipping, and the mums,
Sunday, the muffin man rings his bell,
Sunday tea, cockles, and winkles,
Come out of their shell,
The safety pin does the trick,
It makes the winkles easy to pick.

Newspapers come in handy,
Cut into squares, and placed on a hook,
Also the Beano and Dandy,
While on the toilet, one could
Read a book.

Summer days so much fun,
A picnic packed, a wave to Mum,
Baby in pram, two children by the side,
Thirteen, and in charge of three,
To the park for swings, and slides,
No worry Mum, we'll be home for tea.

Memories, memories, never fade away,
This all seems like only yesterday,
When life was safe and carefree,
Let our tomorrows, be like our yesterdays,
Let's try you and me.

S Kellett

My Childhood Days

Many years ago in my childhood days,
Things were different in many ways,
There were no such things as televisions,
Or fridges in which to keep your provisions.

No children owned expensive toys,
So games were played by girls and boys.
If you were very lucky and had a bike
You would not always have to hike.

At five years old it was the rule,
For children to attend the Village School,
As I was no exception, I too had to go,
Which really did upset me so.

As soon as our lessons were over,
We thought we were in clover,
And homeward we would run,
Change our clothes, and have some fun.

We'd wander down the country lane,
Until we found a nice deep drain,
Where some tadpoles we might catch,
Or even frogspawn ready to hatch.

As we never had much money,
Or lived in a land of milk and honey.
Maybe you do not agree,
But those were the good old days for me.

Irene Morris

CHILDHOOD MEMORIES

The ice cream man with his tricycle
Who came along our street
Sold 'Snofrutes' for a penny,
To us it was a treat.

Going for sweets on a Saturday
With a penny we could buy
A sherbet dab and sucker
Or other sweets to try.

The ragman with his trumpet
Would give you a balloon
For two jam jars or an old wool coat.
We hoped he'd come back soon.

We'd play games and do skipping
With special skipping rhymes
These didn't cost us anything,
But we had happy times.

Just meeting friends out on our street,
Few cars then, happy days,
These simple pleasures now are gone
And lost in memory's haze.

No tops and whips and marbles
Can ever now be seen
As children sit, gaze glassy-eyed
At a computer screen.

No games of tig or football because of parking cars,
They sit and shoot at aliens from Jupiter and Mars.
Perhaps one day when fuel runs out,
Once more they'll have the fun
Of all the games that once we knew and play out in the sun.

Margaret B Baguley

NOW AND THEN

How I would love to turn back time
When life seemed unhurried, more sublime
Where people mattered, communities cared;
We had time for one another, our problems shared.

Even time itself seemed to go much slower,
We only blink now and have lost an hour
No time to relax: stroll along a leafy lane
Work, then more work, until we go insane.

Childhood memories that seemed so sweet
Endless hours of freedom, no malice we'd meet
We roamed free in the woods, played in the park,
Sauntered home for tea, as it began to get dark.

Children today can't go out alone, or run free
For fear of abduction, even murder, how can this be?
Why have things changed in the last twenty years
Where both old and young have to live with these fears?

Some aspects of change I can see as a gain
But morals and values have gone down the drain
Oh to live in a world with no trouble or strife
That must be the ultimate hope of each given life.

Maggy Copeland

HERE'S TO THE NEXT TIME

'Here's to the next time,'
Henry Hall is leading
'Here's to the next time,'
Another show completing.
I hear his music,
With tunes sublime,
In mood nostalgic,
Step back in time.
There is my mother,
Evening meal preparing,
Then, home comes Father,
A cheerful smile he's wearing.
So very clearly,
I see them all,
Those I loved dearly,
Hear Henry Hall.

D J Price

CHILDHOOD MEMORIES

Oh, to be young again having lots of fun,
Back to the good old days,
Not much money, but lots of love
Would always come our way.

Twopence to the movies, only once a week,
Greatest films of all were shown there,
Penny for an ice cream, penny for the bus,
You got a great day out for fourpence, anywhere.

We all went potato picking on the local farms,
I even took a turn picking coal with my dad,
The kids of today would be lost without their laptops
Can you wonder why they think *we are mad*?

I used to love the evening times,
Having to take turns in the tin bath by the fire,
Listening to the music on the wireless before bedtime
Made you feel comfy, cosy and tired.

They don't have fun like that any more,
Life is all study and nightlife,
Not enough simple fun times,
Far too much stress and strife.

Vera Ewers

RADIO COMEDY FROM THE PAST

Harry Secombe, Peter Sellers and Spike Milligan were The Goons,
The Ray Ellington Quartet played a couple of tunes,
Some of the characters in the show were Bluebottle, Eccles,
　　　　　　Neddie Seagoon and Major Bloodnock,
Also on the radio was the half-hour that belonged to Hancock,
With Sid James, Kenneth Williams and Bill Kerr,
And of course Hattie Jacques, we can't forget her.

There was fun with Jimmy Clitheroe, he was very small,
Norman Evans was gossiping to his neighbour, Over The Garden Wall.

Ray's A Laugh starred Kitty Bluett and Ted Ray,
Educating Archie was on every Sunday around midday,
Archie Andrews was a dummy, Peter Brough was a ventriloquist,
Beryl Reid and Max Bygraves were on his guest list.

There was Take It From Here, with Jimmy Edwards, Dick Bentley and
　　　　　　June Whitfield, they were very good,
Late on June was in The News Hudd Lines, with comedian Roy Hudd.

The Al Read Show was recorded in Manchester,
There was the show starring Cheerful Charlie Chester.

The Frankie Howard Show featured Gladys Morgan,
A tiny Welsh comedienne,
Kenneth Horne was in Round The Horne and Beyond Our Ken.

Bebe Daniels and Ben Lyon were in Life With The Lyons,
With their daughter Barbara and Richard their son,
All of these comedy series gave listeners pleasure and fun.

Dave Birkinshaw

FOUND

We knelt in the grass
Barbara and I
searching each blade for the treasure.

It was a warm spring day
the honey bee in the clover buzzing close
and the call of the cuckoo from across the field.

Painstakingly we looked,
time stood still.

A call for tea which we ignored
and then, oh bliss
I gave a shout
triumphant
I had found
a four leaf clover.

Elizabeth Taylor

NAN AND GRANDAD'S HOUSE

In spring came a carpet of bluebells,
The apple trees bloomed, buds showing pink and white.
Snowdrops and daffodils swayed in the breeze.
Every morning such a magical sight.
Summer brought the fruits, apples, pears and cherries.
The fragrance of roses clinging to the wall.
Walk on to the cottage with its shiny door.
Inside I would find the greatest sight of all.
There was Nan in her apron,
Curls in her fine grey hair.
By the fire, swaying gently,
There sat Grandad in his rocking chair.
I remember Nan's sweet smile and welcoming arms.
Grandad's greeting was a bear-like hug.
Then the taste of fresh baked rolls,
And tea in my own special mug.
The childhood carefree memories,
Forever locked in my heart.
I never thought that it could end,
But passing time took us apart.
So long ago and now I greet,
The grandchildren of my own.
Sharing their secrets, their hopes and dreams.
Creating memories for when they are grown.

Joy Cooke

MEMORIES PAST

A cycle ride along the lanes
to places we all know,
the bluebell woods, the beaches
where we played so long ago.
We'd have a picnic, laugh a lot,
the day would pass along,
then we'd cycle five miles home again
before the light was gone.
the next day we would pick wild flowers,
make daisy chains to wear,
they looked so very pretty
when we twined them through our hair.
We'd watch the steam trains puffing by
at times they went quite slow,
we'd stand astride our bikes
and wave to folk we didn't know,
they usually waved back to us
or gave a cheery smile,
then we'd mount our saddles once again
to ride another mile.
Nostalgic, happy days gone by,
so carefree, spent and lazy,
it's difficult to place them now,
as life seems much more crazy.
But memories will never die,
I think it's right to say
that I'm grateful for the life we had,
Oh what they've *missed* today!

Margaret Hanning

DOWN THE DITCHES 1930S

I walked the drainage ditch you know,
in secret, six foot six below
In summer time when ditch was dry
Never met a soul, nor did I try
Down to our ash, swing from its bole
And drop down plop into my hole.

What treasure would I find today?
Foxglove tall as my dad I'd say.
Robin's nest beneath blue forage
Mole just out of ground to forage
Last year inside a blackened pole
Bluetits had nested in a hole.

At the corner I must beware
Perhaps Bert Shore is standing there
Gun in hand, a fearsome chap
What he can't shoot he'll surely trap
I'd walk the length of Grandpa's edge
Then Wills field ditch beneath their hedge.

I love the ditches' steep green banks,
Tall weeds and flowers grow in ranks
Can't hear if Mother calls me in
She'll say I'm bad and live to sin
Blackberries scratch my chin and knees
Old nettles sting me where they please.

I've got to rub on dock again
Or I shall surely die of pain
I've gone and torn my trouser seat
Grandma will mend it, she won't beat
I'm tired now I've had no lunch
I must get back I've got a hunch - they called me.

Dirty shirt and muddy boots
And yet I couldn't give two hoots.
I'm bleeding.

Denis Pentlow

IVY COTTAGE

Our first home was a cottage
When we were newly wed.
A pump in the kitchen
And for the 'loo' just a shed.

So it was 'out in the garden.'
If you needed to 'go'
And to pump water at all -
Don't let the primer get low.

If you have let this happen
Then it's the stream in the lane,
None too hygienic -
But we survived all the same!

Baths, a zinc tub in the kitchen,
Each kettle and pot on the boil,
And it's a case of quick in and out.
To empty that tub -what a toil.

One day we dropped it en route,
And water poured over our feet.
Not made any safer at all -
The oven was open for heat.

I do know the bedroom was cosy,
But icy on a cold winter morn.
Still we were young and so happy
All this could easily be borne.

After nine months we had to move on
To a house better in many ways,
But thoughts of our cottage remind us
Of some of our happiest days.

Joan Chapman

ANCHOR BOOKS
SUBMISSIONS INVITED
SOMETHING FOR EVERYONE

ANCHOR BOOKS GEN - Any subject, light-hearted clean fun, nothing unprintable please.

THE OPPOSITE SEX - Have your say on the opposite gender. Do they drive you mad or can we co-exist in harmony?

THE NATURAL WORLD - Are we destroying the world around us? What should we do to preserve the beauty and the future of our planet - you decide!

All poems no longer than 30 lines.
Always welcome! No fee!
Plus cash prizes to be won!

Mark your envelope (eg *The Natural World*)
And send to:
Anchor Books
Remus House, Coltsfoot Drive
Peterborough, PE2 9JX

**OVER £10,000 IN POETRY PRIZES
TO BE WON!**

Send an SAE for details on our New Year 2002 competition!